EAST MEETS WEST

Traditional *and* Contemporary Asian Dishes *from* Acclaimed

Vancouver Restaurants

STEPHANIE YUEN

EAST MEETS WEST

Douglas & McIntyre
D&M Publishers Inc.
Vancouver/Toronto/Berkeley

Douglas & McIntyre
An imprint of D&M Publishers Inc.
2323 Quebec Street, Suite 201
Vancouver BC Canada V5T 4S7
www.douglas-mcintyre.com

Cataloguing data available from
Library and Archives Canada
ISBN 978-1-55365-863-4 (pbk.)
ISBN 978 1 55365 864 1 (ebook)

Editing by Lucy Kenward
Copy editing by Iva Cheung
Cover and interior design by Naomi MacDougall
Cover photographs by John Sherlock
Principal photography by John Sherlock
Secondary photography by Naomi MacDougall
Printed and bound in China by
C&C Offset Printing Co., Ltd.
Text printed on acid-free paper
Distributed in the U.S. by Publishers Group West

We gratefully acknowledge the financial support of the
Canada Council for the Arts, the British Columbia Arts
Council, the Province of British Columbia through the
Book Publishing Tax Credit and the Government of Canada
through the Canada Book Fund for our publishing activities.

CONTENTS

I DEVELOPED AN interest in food at a very young age, and like many food lovers, I started learning about cooking by watching my mom. I remember as a seven-year-old standing on a stool in the tiny kitchen of our 400-square-foot apartment in Kowloon, Hong Kong, fiddling with ladles and turners as she showed me the fun and the magic of authentic Hakka home cooking. Bubbling away on one of our two stove elements would be a pot of trotters, while on the other she'd be wok-frying sliced beef while chopping up a perfectly cooked soy chicken that I'd helped her slaughter and pluck. Minutes later, she would turn out a large platter of stir-fried choy sum and mushrooms she'd bought fresh that morning at the market.

By the time I first set foot in British Columbia in the spring of 1975, I had eaten my fair share of Asian food in Hong Kong, and I was impressed by how fresh and tasty the food was in Vancouver's Chinatown. Buyers bustled among the fishmongers selling live seafood, and I readily inhaled the oven-fresh scent wafting down the street from the bakery cafés and the mouthwatering smell of grilled meat escaping from the meat shops. It didn't take me long to fall in love with Dollar Meat's barbecued ducks, Sunrise Soya Foods' tofu and Hon's hor fan rice noodles. The lineups at restaurants were constant, and I was happy to join them.

My eldest brother, Tony, was the manager of Kingsland Chinese Restaurant on Granville Street at the time, and he took me inside the eatery's huge kitchen. There I vividly remember the owner and chef, Raymond Leung, standing in front of a humongous wok, his quick hands turning raw sticky rice, as he cooked it with diced lap chong (sausages), dried shrimp and mushrooms, and his forehead dripping with sweat. In another section of the kitchen, cooks stacked bamboo baskets filled with hand-crafted dumplings, stuffed buns, seasoned spareribs, chicken feet and tofu rolls, ready to be steamed as the dim sum orders came in. By the deep fryer, other staff dipped spring rolls and salt-and-pepper squid into the sea of hot oil until the outer layers turned crispy and golden. It was my first time in such a large, busy kitchen, and I was dazzled by the intensity of the tastes and sights and smells. I immediately wanted to learn more about the many aspects of Chinese food and cooking.

It was another few years before I was granted landed-immigrant status and had the chance to return to Vancouver to eat in the city's restaurants and observe how its multicultural culinary scene had metamorphosed. Although Asian immigration to Canada dates back nearly two centuries to the 1870s and '80s, when the Chinese (mostly Taishanese-speaking people from Guangdong Province) were imported as labourers for the railroads and the Japanese came to fish the Pacific waters and log the coastal forests, there were few restaurants back then. The earliest ones were Chinese smorgasbords started by the Cantonese cooks who fed the millworkers around what is now Gastown in the 1870s, but most Vancouverites were eating only what they prepared at home.

By the late 1950s and early '60s, a few restaurants throughout Vancouver had been serving "Chinese and Western Food." Several Chinese eateries such as Dragon Inn, The Rickshaw, Mandarin Gardens, Asian Garden, Ming's, HoHo and Marco Polo Supper Club had opened around Main, Pender and Columbia, and, driven by an influx of immigrants from Hong Kong beginning in the late 1960s, Chinatown was officially declared a historic site in 1970. These newcomers injected vital energy into Chinatown, and, by opening a number of retail shops, grocery stores and restaurants, successfully made it a destination for all things Asian.

The first wholly Chinese eatery to expand beyond Chinatown was Flamingo Chinese Restaurant, which opened in a residential area at Cambie and West 59th in 1973. Today, the restaurant continues to provide both traditional and modern Chinese cuisine in a cozy dining room at the very same location. The following year the grand seven-hundred-seat Kingsland Chinese Restaurant was opened downtown. A team of four chefs came from Hong Kong to showcase their culinary talents and enchant Vancouver diners with trendy Hong Kong–style dishes served in a lavishly decorated room. Today, three of these four chefs are still cooking in Vancouver.

Next door to Chinatown, in the area around Powell Street and Gore, Japantown started to flourish. Professional chefs were hired from Japan, and among the first authentic restaurants to open its doors was Aki Japanese Restaurant, whose simple English menu offered sushi, sashimi, noodles and teriyaki. A nostalgic Japanese menu was posted on the walls. The first Fujiya Japanese food store followed in 1977. It wasn't long before other Asian stores and restaurants popped up: the first Korean restaurant, the Korean Barbeque Restaurant, was established on East Hastings Street, and Indian eateries appeared on Main, Fraser and Kingsway.

The major turning point for Vancouver's Asian communities, though, was Expo 86. Waves of Vietnamese refugees and immigrants from Hong Kong flowed into Metro Vancouver, followed by Taiwanese and Korean émigrés. Beginning in 1990, Canada significantly increased its immigration levels, which attracted Malaysians, Singaporeans, Nepalese, Filipinos, Thais, Cambodians and Laotians, who have made the West Coast their new home.

Overnight, neighbourhoods changed, and restaurants popped up in previously unexpected locations. The original Japantown succumbed to rapid social changes, but Japanese restaurants blossomed along Robson, Burrard and Alberni Streets and other parts of town. Vietnamese noodle houses appeared along Hastings and Kingsway in East Vancouver, while Thai restaurants cropped up downtown and in Richmond. Taiwanese bubble tea cafés, many of them open late, became popular hangouts in Burnaby and Richmond.

The opening of the mighty Dynasty Chinese Restaurant in the Meridian Hotel on Hastings Street in 1988 signalled a new era of Asian cooking in the city. A team of five top-notch chefs from Hong Kong was brought to Vancouver to give locals and visitors the *crème de la crème* of luxurious Chinese dining experiences in a room that was elegantly designed, offered an enchanting ambiance and impeccable service and served exquisite cuisine. Unfortunately, the Meridian Hotel was relocated a few years later, and the extravagant Dynasty Chinese Restaurant was closed. Four of the five chefs, however, chose to stay in Vancouver, including Master Hung, the maestro of traditional Chinese barbecue, who now runs his own family-style barbecue restaurant in Richmond.

Along with the expanding Asian population and the profusion of restaurants came more and more Asian grocery stores and markets in different parts of the city. T&T, the first Asian supermarket to open in Canada, planted its store at the corner of Cambie and No. 3 Road in Richmond, which by 1993 was already the nucleus of Asian shopping centres and strip malls. Within a few years, Richmond became known as the "New Chinatown," "Little Asia" or "Little Hong Kong" and still attracts a steady flow of immigrants from Taiwan and Mainland China who have continued to arrive since 2000.

Today, despite the fact that Toronto has a larger Asian population than Vancouver, this city is home to Canada's most vibrant Asian culinary community. Gone is the era of Chinese smorgasbord and Chinese-Canadian restaurants, when chop suey, deep-fried prawns, egg foo yung and sweet-and-sour pork ruled the menus. Instead, as diners travel widely and become more educated, they demand more authentic dishes, and restaurants are turning out food similar to what's being served "back home." Woks, bamboo steamers and rice cookers are now widely stocked and found even in non-Asian kitchens, and a range of previously unavailable seasonings and herbs and sauces is easier and easier to find. Judging by the proficiency of non-Asians' handling chopsticks, ordering confidently in Asian restaurants and distinguishing second-rate fare from fresh, well-prepared dishes, Vancouverites are committed to Asian cuisine! Further proof lies in the hundreds of sushi and sashimi bars, izakayas and noodle houses (pho' restaurants now existing in greater numbers than any other kind of eatery in Vancouver), tandoori kitchens and dim sum restaurants, as well as the city's first artisan sake maker.

It's exciting to see so many European- and/or American-trained chefs using Asian ingredients and cooking techniques to create unique Asian-inspired dishes made with local, seasonal produce. As Mark Schatzker wrote in *Condé Nast Traveler*, "Vancouver now produces the best Chinese food in the world," and, I would argue, the best *Asian* food on the planet.

ACKNOWLEDGEMENTS

EMBARKING ON THIS cookbook has been a dream come true. It has not only taken me on an amazing cultural and culinary journey but has also given me the chance to work with some of the city's best chefs—both a fulfilling and a humbling experience!

Allow me to express my gratitude to the important folks behind this book. First of all to my mom, who allowed me into the kitchen not just to watch but to get my hands dirty helping her cook. From her I learned how to make delicious homestyle soup from scratch and how to use clay pots to make stews, and I witnessed first-hand how serving lovingly prepared dishes brings people together. To my brother Tony, who led me into the wonderland of Chinese restaurants and ethnic cuisine and inspired a career in food writing. To my husband, Henry, who never says no to any food adventure—be it overseas or down the street, cooking in or dining out, rustic or gourmet. He approaches every meal with a smile and a great appetite.

To my taste testers—Athen, Deanna, Anthio, Kendra and our next-door neighbours, Erin and Karl—who are always ready to sample new things and whose discerning palates, healthy appetites and honest opinions helped make this book better. To Joan and Sid Cross, for their words of encouragement and for keeping my spirits high and maintaining my confidence when I needed it most.

And to my editor, Lucy Kenward, and her brilliant and patient team at Douglas & McIntyre, for believing in me, guiding me and working with me through the book-publishing process.

Last but not least, I salute all the chefs who shared their culinary skills and delectable recipes. You are the heart and soul, the pride and joy of Metro Vancouver's glorious Asian culinary world.

ASIAN SPICES

Ajwain (Carom) Often mistaken for celery seeds, these tiny, light-brown to red seeds are related to caraway and cumin and have a strong thyme-like flavour. They are used for medicinal purposes and to make essential oils but also complement fish and starchy foods.

Asafoetida An Indian spice derived from giant resinous fennel plants, raw asafoetida has a sharp sulphuric odour that becomes a mild truffle flavour when cooked. It is good with vegetable dishes and sauces, but use only a tiny amount at a time.

Asian sweet basil (Thai basil) Slightly serrated and shiny dark green leaves on a purple stem, this herb adds a hidden hint of scented cloves and licorice. It can be used as a garnish for almost any Thai dish and adds aroma to salads and noodle dishes.

Cardamom Native to India, cardamom are spicy brown or black seeds found inside hard-shelled green pods. Both have a pungent aroma and a subtle sweet flavour that is vital to garam masala and curry powders.

Cassia bark (Chinese cinnamon) Native to Burma and a relative of cinnamon, cassia is a bright-yellow tree bark with a thicker texture and less aromatic fragrance than cinnamon. It is used mostly with savoury dishes and is one of the main original ingredients in five-spice powder. When a Chinese recipe calls for cinnamon, it usually means cassia bark; the two are interchangeable.

Cilantro (Coriander, Chinese parsley) Often used as a garnish or a seasoning, this leafy, green herb has thin stems with clusters of petal-like serrated leaves and a unique flavour that is sometimes described as slightly soapy. In culinary circles, the fresh plant is known as cilantro, its dried seeds as coriander.

Cinnamon This aromatic tree bark is more brown than its relative, cassia bark, and comes in sticks or as a powder. Chinese consider cinnamon a valuable medicinal herb, and in its ground form it is one of the essential elements of most Asian five-spice powders.

Cloves These dried flower buds from the evergreen clove tree look like tiny spikes and have a very peppery and cinnamony smell. Cloves are used whole or ground, in sweet and savoury dishes.

Coriander seeds Harvested from a plant in the carrot family, these seeds are usually dried and used either whole or ground. They impart a nutty, lemony flavour. See also Cilantro.

Cumin seeds These seeds come from a plant related to parsley and have a strong, warm aroma and a distinctive flavour that is used throughout Southeast Asian cooking. Whole or ground, cumin is often paired with coriander to spice curries.

Curry leaves These small green leaves come from a tropical tree that belongs to the citrus family. They add a warm "curry" flavour to food. Fresh curry leaves still attached to their tiny stems are more fragrant than dried ones, but both are tough and should be removed from the dish before serving.

Fennel seeds These seeds have an anise flavour and a grassy texture. They are usually used in savoury recipes.

Fenugreek Fenugreek is native to Asia and southern Europe, and both its fresh green leaves (methi) and dried seeds are used in cooking. The seeds are mildly sweet with a subtle bitter flavour and a nutty aroma and are often combined with other spices in a sauce. The leaves are often cooked with root vegetables.

Five-spice powder Many chefs now develop their own five-spice powders, and the name has become a common term for any blend of five Asian spices; however, the authentic version comes from China and is a blend of equal parts of ground cassia bark (or cinnamon), cloves, fennel seeds, star anise and Szechuan peppercorns.

Galangal (Blue ginger, Laos, Galanga) A rhizome that belongs to the ginger family, galangal is lighter coloured, tighter skinned and has a more robust, slightly peppery flavour than common ginger. Greater galangal, a native of Java, is from a bigger, taller ginger plant and is a key ingredient in Thai and Indonesian dishes, while lesser galangal, which originated in China, is from a smaller, shorter plant and is used to flavour beverages.

Garam masala A blend of dry-roasted ground spices commonly used in northern Indian cooking and believed to warm the palate and lift the spirits. Many variations exist, but most include cinnamon and cloves.

Ginger (Shoga, Jiang or Geung) This edible root of the ginger plant is irregularly shaped with a light-brown skin. Its flesh is crisp and yellow when fresh and adds a unique spicy note to any dish. Ginger is always used fresh in Asian cooking, not dried and ground as commonly used in Western cooking. Look for smooth skins, juicy flesh and a strong aroma; avoid ginger that is woody, fibrous and dry.

Ichimi (Togarashi) Small Japanese hot red chili peppers, available in specialty grocery stores.

Kinome The young, tender leaves of the ash tree, which are serrated and prickly; they have a subtle mint flavour and are used in Japan for garnishing and seasoning.

Mitsuba (Honeywort, Japanese chervil)

Lemon grass This yellowish-green, tightly packed foot-long stem is indeed a kind of grass that looks like a green onion but with a more rigid stalk. Sold in bunches loosely tied with an elastic, it has a woody texture and a herbal lemony fragrance that is commonly used in teas, soups and curries. Look for fresh, firm stalks: the lower part should be white and the upper leaves should be jade green but not crusty. Discard the outer leaves and the root part of the bulb before cooking with it.

Mace The lacy, papery red covering (aril) of the nutmeg seed, which is ground and used as a sweet and fragrant spice.

Mango powder (Amchoor, Amchur) Widely used in Indian cooking is this spice made from unripe mangoes that have been sun-dried and ground to a powder. It adds a tangy and slightly sweet flavour to the dish.

Mint The leaves of this flowering shrub are often used in cooking, either fresh or dried and then ground. It imparts a slightly sweet flavour with a cool aftertaste that is popular in teas and desserts and as a garnish for savoury dishes.

Mitsuba (Honeywort, Japanese chervil) This celery-flavoured plant, which looks like flat-leaf parsley, is used as a seasoning for soups and salads and also as a garnish.

Mustard seeds These tiny round yellow, black or brown seeds of the mustard plant have a warm, nutty flavour and are used for seasoning and for making spice blends.

Ngu vi huong This Vietnamese five-spice powder, which is used in seasonings and marinades, consists of cloves, cinnamon, fennel seed, licorice and star anise.

Nutmeg Shaped like a dry, wrinkly brown olive, this hard seed of the nutmeg tree is used for braising and making soup stocks. Ground nutmeg is used as a spice, often in soups and stocks.

Orange peel The peel of sun-dried tangerines, this wrinkled brown spice has a mild peppery flavour and a strong citrus fragrance. It is used in both sweet and savoury recipes.

Peppercorns Native to Southeast Asia, peppercorns are the world's oldest and most widely used spice and add heat to any dish. The only true peppercorns are black, green and white. Green peppercorns, a rare find in North America, are the fresh green berries of the pepper plant; black peppercorns are hand-picked green berries fermented for a few days, then sun-dried to become wrinkled and dark; white peppercorns are ripe berries first soaked in water to loosen their skins, then dried, after the skins have been rubbed off. *Szechuan (Sichuan) peppercorns* are the round reddish-brown berries of prickly ash trees and have a slightly lemony taste that numbs the palate, and *pink peppercorns (baies roses)* are dried berries native to South America.

Shiso (Chinese basil, Japanese basil) This serrated, spade-shaped leaf of the perilla plant belongs to the mint and basil family and has an intense minty flavour and a sweet, nutty aroma. It is often used as a garnish.

Shichimi togarashi A spicy Japanese condiment consisting of seven ingredients: red chili flakes, sansho (Szechuan peppercorns), white sesame seeds, nori flakes, crushed dried mandarin peels, black hemp seeds and white poppy seeds. It is used with soups and noodle dishes.

Star anise A small, hard star-shaped spice pod full of seeds that comes from a small evergreen tree native to China, this is a key component of five-spice powder.

Tamarind (Imli, Indian date) This pod of a bushy tree native to North Africa is widely grown in South Asia. Four to five inches long with a hard brown shell, the tamarind pod is cracked open for its mushy but acidic sweet-and-sour brown pulp, which is often made into a paste. It is used to season soups, stews, noodle dishes, drinks and desserts.

Thai chili A small inch-long very hot green chili pepper that turns red when fully ripe. When dried, it is called bird's eye chili.

Turmeric (Yellow ginger) A relative of ginger that is native to China, this spice is boiled, dried and then ground into a yellow-orange powder with a musky, almost bitter flavour. The raw spice has a harsh gritty texture and should be cooked. It is an essential component in curry dishes.

ASIAN VEGETABLES AND LEGUMES

Arrowroot A small, round, beige-skinned tuber that is crunchy when raw but starchy when cooked. The powdered form is used as a thickening agent for puddings, sauces and other cooked foods.

Azuki (adzuki) beans These small, dried russet-coloured beans have a white line along one side. They are often boiled with sugar to make red bean paste, which is a popular filling for Asian buns and other pastries.

Bamboo shoots The edible young shoots of certain bamboo plants, they are sold in fresh, dried and canned versions. The round, fat shoots with scale-like skins are the winter shoots, whereas the thin, green horn-like shoots are harvested in the spring and summer. Use them to add crunchy texture and a sweet nutty flavour.

Banana blossoms (Banana flowers) The palm-size young flowers of the banana tree grow at the end of the stem holding the cluster of bananas and look like large purple buds. The outer layers are removed and the slightly bitter flower is used fresh to flavour salads and stews. Fresh flowers can also be deep-fried or dried.

Banana leaves Although inedible, these broad green leaves with a slight anise scent are used to wrap food for steaming, for cooking or for short-distance travel. They also stand in for plates. Buy them fresh or frozen; thaw frozen leaves, and soak or boil fresh ones in water before using to prevent them from cracking.

Bean sprouts Most beans can be sprouted, but the sprouts of mung beans are the ones most often enjoyed as a vegetable. They are slender, white, 2- to 3-inch-long threads protruding from a tiny green-capped bean. Although mild-tasting, raw sprouts add texture and crunch to many dishes. Grow your own, or buy them very fresh and use them immediately, as they quickly become soggy.

Bitter melon (Bitter gourd) Two varieties are commonly used— one for Chinese cooking and one for Indian cuisine. Chinese bitter melons are cucumber shaped and have lumpy green skin and off-white sponge-like flesh with red seeds. Indian bitter melons are smaller and greener and have spiky skins. Both the skin and flesh are edible. To reduce the bitterness, soak the sliced melon in salted water for 15 minutes before adding it to any recipe.

Bitter melon

Bok choy An Asian vegetable related to cabbage, this winter-hardy vegetable has long, smooth dark green leaves with thick white stems. *Baby bok choy* are the small sprouts with a more delicate flavour. Both are best used in stir fries, braises, soups, stews and steamed; they are rarely eaten raw. *Shanghai bok choy* is very similar in size and shape to baby bok choy but is jade green all over.

Burdock root (Gobo) The taproot of young burdock plants is harvested as a root vegetable. It is very crisp and has a sweet, mellow but distinct flavour with a harshness that can be removed by soaking the root in water for 5 to 10 minutes. Once sliced, this root can be boiled, sautéed and made into soup. Dried gobo is an essential root for medicinal use.

Chinese cabbage (Siu choy, Hakusai) Similar to napa cabbage, this variety is longer and thinner with yellowish-green leaves and a mild flavour. It is popular in soups, stir fries and Korean kimchi.

Chinese celery (Kun choy) Often cooked with leeks or in stir fries and soups, this dark green vegetable has thin celery-like stems and leaves that resemble parsley. Unlike regular celery, it has a strong herbal flavour.

Chinese ears A Chinese herbal term that refers to six particular edible fungi families—cloud ears (including tree/wood ears), guihua ears, silver ears, stone ears, yellow ears and yue ears.

Chinese leeks (Gou choy) These long, flat, ¼-inch-wide leeks look like grass and have a rustic, earthy flavour. Before they are harvested, young leeks are stored in the dark for a few days until they turn yellow. Called yellow chives (gou wong), they have a stronger flavour and are used in thick soups cooked with duck or crabmeat.

Chinese long beans (Dau gok) At about a foot long, these slender beans are much longer than common green beans. Choose crisp, tender, young beans, and cook them in stir fries or egg foo yung.

Chinese mustard (Gai choy) This popular green, leafy vegetable has seeds, leaves and thin stems that are edible. A member of the mustard family, it is used fresh, preserved with salt or pickled. Young plants are less pungent than more mature ones. Shi-li-hon is a thinner-stemmed, leafier vegetable that belongs to the same family. Both are preserved and pickled in the northern part of China.

Chinese okra (Si gua) Most people know this plant as a loofah, the dried sponge used to rub dead skin from their bodies, but when the vegetable is young, it is eaten in many parts of Asia. Its rough, dark green skin and lengthwise ridges encase soft, white flesh with a delicate flavour. Unlike regular okra, it is tender rather than mushy when cooked. Look for firm, blemish-free vegetables.

Chinese onions (King onions, Rakkyo) A variety of wild onion with long, slender green shoots that taper to a delicate white bulb. It has a milder flavour than common green onions. In Japan, the bulbs are often pickled in vinegar and served as a side dish. A common way of preparing Chinese onions (and green onions) for cooking and garnishing is to shred them by finely slicing them on the bias.

Choy sum (Yu choy) A very popular green vegetable, choy sum has dark green stems and oval leaves. It literally means "vegetable heart," referring to its tender leaves. Stir-fry or blanch the leaves on their own, or serve them as a side dish.

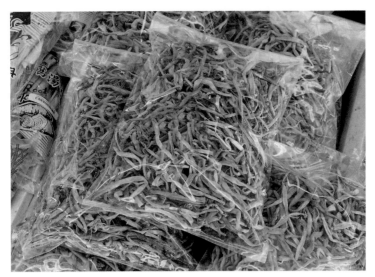

Dried lily buds (Golden needles, Tiger lily buds)

Cloud ears A floret-shaped, grey-black fungus, cloud ears are valued for their crunchy texture. They have little flavour of their own but soak up flavours around them and are a main ingredient in moo shu pork and chicken hot pot. Buy dried cloud ears loose or in plastic bags, keep them in an airtight container for up to a year and soak them in warm water for at least 15 minutes before using them. Rinse the cloud ears, cut off and discard the tough stems and cook them according to the recipe.

Daikon (Asian radish, Lo bok) This versatile, white root vegetable looks like a large carrot with crisp, juicy flesh and a mild radish flavour. Use it in soups or stir fries, pickle it or eat it raw.

Dal (Dhal) The Hindi term for dried pulses (leguminous crops), such as peas, beans and lentils.

Dried lily buds (Golden needles, Tiger lily buds) This earthy, slightly musky-tasting seasoning is made from the dried unopened buds of the tiger lily flower, which look like a large, thick, golden-yellow needles. The most flavourful buds are pale but not brittle; cut off a quarter inch at the bottom, then soak the buds in water for about 30 minutes before using them.

Eggplants This heavy purple-skinned nightshade fruit is native to India and has white flesh and small brown seeds. *Japanese eggplants* (also known as Chinese eggplants) are longer and narrower and lighter purple than Indian eggplants. They are also thinner skinned and less bitter than their Indian counterparts. *Thai eggplants* are small and round and range in colour from white to green to striped varieties with a firm and crunchy texture.

Enoki (Enokidake, Enokitake) These cultivated clumps of white mushrooms have thin 5- to 6-inch-long stalks and tiny caps. They are very mild tasting but have a lovely crisp texture. Look for firm, white, shiny caps and stems.

Gai lan (Chinese broccoli) Similar in taste and texture to regular broccoli, gai lan has longer, thinner stalks and glossy blue-green leaves rather than florets. It is popular fried with ginger and garlic.

Garlic chives (Chinese chives) Similar to green chives, garlic chives are dark green, with long and slender stems and a light-green bud at the end. They are crunchier than leeks.

Ginkgo nuts Inside the inedible fruit of the maidenhair tree indigenous to China are these nutty seeds, whose hard, off-white shell looks like a pistachio. Once soaked and sun-dried, these seeds are used for medicinal purposes and for cooking. Eat the nuts sparingly, as they contain potent allergens that can cause discomfort. Ginkgo nuts are sold in Chinese herbal stores and Asian supermarkets, either whole or in shells, canned, dried or vacuum packed.

Hairy melon (Mo gua, Jit gua) A heavy zucchini-like vegetable with a green, hairy skin and firm, white, mild-flavoured flesh. Scrape the thin skin with a flat knife to remove it. Use it in stir fries, soups or braised stews.

Jicama The edible part of this enormous plant is the root, which is light brown and papery on the outside but creamy white on the inside. Jicama is crunchy and firm like Asian pears, with a sweet, starchy flavour; it can be eaten raw or cooked.

Ji chai (Shepherd's purse) A wild dandelion-like vegetable native to Shanghai. Available fresh in the spring, it has a mild spinach flavour and is now in such high demand that it is being cultivated. It is available in frozen packages in some Chinese markets. Use it as you would spinach.

Kaffir limes Rounder, much smaller and bumpier-skinned than common limes, the kaffirs are less juicy but have a more aromatic scent. The leaves (fresh or dried) and the rind are more frequently used for cooking than the fruit itself.

Ginkgo nuts

Lentils These seeds of the lentil plant are loaded with protein and are an important meat substitute for vegetarians. Most common are the dark brown, green and orange-brown varieties. *Urad dal* are slow-cooking black lentils from South Asia with a creamy white flesh. Serve them as a side dish, or add them to salads, stews, soups and even desserts. Lentils must be soaked or boiled before eating.

Lotus leaves Whether fresh or dried, these huge round leaves are mostly used, like banana leaves, for steaming or serving food. They impart a unique scented flavour to food and are sometimes used in soup. Soak the leaves in warm water for an hour before using them to make them easier to handle.

Lotus root (Hasu, Renkon) The flowers, seeds, young shoots and rhizomes of the lotus plant are all edible. When sliced in cross-section, the peach-coloured roots look like cart wheels. Crunchy and starchy with a mild flavour, lotus root can be deep-fried, stir-fried, braised or pickled.

Lotus seeds The small, oval, cream-coloured seeds of the lotus plant are starchy and generally made into a paste for dessert fillings.

Matsutake (Pine mushroom) A wild, dark-brown Japanese mushroom with a long stem relative to the size of its cap. It has a firm, meaty texture and a nutty flavour and is particularly prized by the Japanese in soups. A North American variant exists and is more likely to be found in local markets than matsutake imported from Japan.

Mizuna A thin, feathery Japanese mustard green leaf with a delicate flavour that is popular in salad mixes or as a garnish.

Mung beans (Green beans, Moong dal) These tiny oval beans have a green husk that splits in half to reveal yellow flesh. Fresh mung beans are sprouted, and dried beans (split or whole) can be used in soups, stews, salads and curries. Once boiled, the whole beans soften and can be used to make noodles or mung bean paste.

Napa cabbage This cabbage, which originated in China, is a close relative of Chinese cabbage (siu choy) but has lighter green and yellow leaves and firmer, wider white stems.

Pandan leaves (Screwpine leaves) These long, flat blade-like leaves grow in a fanned arrangement on a very upright tropical plant. They have a unique floral aroma and are mostly used to make desserts.

Pea shoots The tender young shoots and tendrils of snow pea vines are harvested before they blossom and used to add crispness to salads and stir fries.

Shallots Like garlic, shallots grow in a cluster of bulbs that make up a head. The reddish-brown outer layer is not eaten, but the firm, light-purple insides are sweeter, milder and more complex in flavour than regular onions.

Shiitake mushrooms These large mushrooms have short, tough stems and large tan or dark-brown spotted caps. They are native to Japan and Korea but are now cultivated in North America. Fresh shiitakes are often used to replace dehydrated Chinese mushrooms (black mushrooms). Soak dried shiitakes in water for at least an hour to rehydrate them. Use them in soups and stews or grill or sauté the fresh ones.

Silver ears (Snow ears) White or beige flower-shaped clusters that look like mesh bath sponges, silver ears are a fungus with a very mild flavour and a crunchy texture that becomes gelatinous when cooked for a long time. It is popular for making soups and vegetarian dishes, as well as desserts.

Snow peas Native to Thailand and Burma, snow peas are eaten pod and all. These crunchy flat green peas are slightly sweet and are usually blanched, steamed or stir-fried to preserve their crispness.

Soy beans (Soya bean, Yellow bean) The fruit of a species of legume with a thousand or more varieties, soy beans are infinitely versatile and are the backbone of many Asian dishes. They are processed to make soy bean oil and tofu and fermented to make soy sauce, bean paste and tempeh. Soy beans can also be sprouted; the result is a thick, long-stemmed white sprout with a yellow nut-like head.

Silver ears (Snow ears)

Straw mushrooms Available fresh in Asia, these small, dense, inch-long (or less) mushrooms have a broad stem and a droopy brown cap. They are often harvested "unpeeled," which means the cap has not completely opened, but these can easily be confused with other veiled mushrooms, including some poisonous ones. They are available dried or canned outside of Asia. Use them in soups, stews and stir fries.

Taiwanese cabbage (Gao-li choy) This variety tastes much like regular green cabbage but has a flat top with thinner, more tender and sweeter leaves.

Taro leaves (Gabi) Dried or fresh, the large heart-shaped taro leaves are very popular in Filipino cooking.

Taro root (Dasheen) The large gourd-like tuber of the taro plant. The yellow-skinned roots are known as dasheen, and the brownish-purple roots are called taro roots. Both are covered in short hairs that irritate human skin, especially when wet, so wear gloves when handling them. Taro must be cooked. Use it for roasting or deep-frying or in stews and soups. It is popular in fondue hot pots, steamed dishes and desserts, and taro flour is used to make dim sum.

Tatsoi (Spinach mustard) These small, dark green, spoon-shaped leaves have a creamy texture and a mild mustard flavour that is delicious raw or cooked.

Tree ears (Wood ears) A relative of cloud ears, this white or black fungus is larger, tougher and crunchier. Shredded black tree ears are a main ingredient in hot and sour soup. Soak the dried fungus in water for 30 minutes before using it.

Water chestnuts These small dark-brown corms are from an aquatic plant found in East Asia. Their firm white flesh is nutty-sweet with a crunchy texture that they retain whether raw, cooked or canned. Use them raw, boiled, grilled and pickled, or dried and ground into flour.

Watercress A dark-green vegetable with palm-shaped leaves that grows in the wild, mostly along dikes and in shallow waters. It has a peppery, tangy, slightly bitter flavour when raw but becomes nutty and sweet when cooked and is favoured for making Chinese soups and hot pots.

Water spinach (Chinese watercress, Hollow vegetable, Ong choy) This aquatic plant with hollow stems and green, almond-shaped leaves grows wild and is considered a noxious weed in North America. Light aqua-green ones grow in water bogs and jade green ones grow on dry land; both are used in cooking.

Winged beans (Goa beans) Fatter, longer versions of common green beans, these are starchier and taste like asparagus. The tender young pods are most commonly used, but the leaves, roots and flowers are also edible.

Winter melon (Wax gourd, Dong gua) Very large with a smooth skin when mature (it is fuzzy when young), this light green, oval-shaped melon has white and spongy flesh with a mild flavour. It is made into drinks and winter melon casserole, which is made by hollowing half the melon to hold and steam soup.

STAPLE INGREDIENTS

Bean sauce (Bean paste) Made from pressed dried or cured beans, this seasoning comes in four varieties. *Ground bean paste* is thick and brown and made with fermented soy beans. It has a sweet toasted nut flavour and is a staple all-purpose seasoning. *Black bean sauce* is made with fermented black beans and is salty, briny and slightly bittersweet. It is used to season Chinese and Filipino dishes. *Garlic and chili bean sauce* is a brown bean sauce spiced with crushed garlic and chilies. Thai, Mandarin and Taiwanese cooks use it as a condiment or a seasoning. *Sweet bean sauce* is the ground bean sauce made with more sugar added and can replace hoisin.

Bean curd (Tofu) Coagulated soy milk that has been pressed into cakes and then cut into squares. It is available in various consistencies, from soft (almost pudding-like) to extra firm (almost meaty). Off-white and mild tasting, bean curd absorbs flavours and is popular as a meat replacement.

Bean curd sheets The condensed layer of "skin" that forms on the surface of heated soy milk. These golden-yellow sheets are processed and packaged as large, moist, oval sheets used for wrapping food; dried, crispy, rectangular sheets used in soups or desserts; and long rolled and deep-fried sticks for stewing and braising.

Bonito flakes Dried, shaved flakes of the firm-textured, moderately oily bonito fish, a member of the mackerel family. (Nowadays, bonito flakes can refer to any dried fish flakes.) They are especially important for making the Japanese broth called dashi.

Breads and buns A staple in many Asian countries. *Naan* is an oval-shaped white or whole wheat bread cooked on the walls of a traditional Indian tandoor oven. *Chapattis* are unleavened Indian round breads made with whole wheat flour and water and cooked on a griddle. *Dosas* are made with rice flour and black lentils. Popular in South India and Sri Lanka, these crispy fermented crêpes are filled with curries and other ingredients. *Roti* is a round, fluffy and thick bread made of whole wheat flour and cooked on a griddle. It is eaten in many Southeast and South Asian countries. *Pappadums* are made from lentil and chickpea flour and are often spiced and served crisp, like a big round hard-shell tortilla. *Steamed buns* (bao) are Chinese buns made with flour, water and yeast then formed into rounds, squares or twists and steamed until they are soft and fluffy. Plain buns or those made with green onions accompany meals; other buns stuffed with savoury or sweet fillings are served as a snack or dessert.

Chili sauce Used in almost every Asian culture, all versions are made with one or more varieties of chili peppers and other ingredients such as bean paste, garlic, vinegar, salt and sugar. Sambal, sriracha, chili bean paste and garlic chili sauce are just a few examples.

Chinese bacon (Chinese preserved pork, Lap yok) Brined, cured, dried and/or smoked, these strips of pork belly are salty with a hint of hoisin. They are often cooked in a rice cooker over steaming rice or chopped and added to stir fries.

Chinese ham Marinated and air-dried whole brined pork hind leg. Although it tastes a lot like prosciutto, it is not consumed raw but is a must-have ingredient for making premium stocks.

Chinese sausages (Lap chong)

Chinese sausages (Lap chong) Ground and seasoned chicken, pork, or pig or duck liver enclosed in a casing, then hung and sun-dried for preservation. These thin, 5- to 6-inch-long sausages must be cooked before eating by steaming them with rice in a cooker or adding them to stir fries or steamed meat dishes.

Dried black olives Pitted, salted, sun-dried and pressed Chinese black olives. Steamed and diced, they are served as a condiment for fried rice or steamed pork or seafood.

Fermented black beans (Douchi) Fermented and salted soy beans used to make black bean sauce. Chinese black beans are dried and packaged in cartons or plastic bags; Filipino black beans also come in cans. Mostly salty, with a slightly bitter and sweet taste, they are used as a seasoning.

Fish sauce (Nam pla, Nuoc mam) A thick, clear brown liquid made from salted and fermented fish, often anchovies or sardines. Robust and intensely flavoured, it is used as a seasoning, marinade or dipping sauce.

Hamm dan (Salty eggs) Raw duck eggs traditionally preserved by being covered in a mixture of brine and clay for at least 3 weeks. Nowadays most of them are made by simply soaking in brine, but flavour and texture are compromised. The hard-boiled eggs are served as a side dish or diced and cooked with vegetables, the raw ones are added to soup or congee; both are salty. The whole yolks are a key ingredient in moon cakes.

Hoisin sauce A thick reddish-brown dipping sauce made with a starch such as sweet potato and flavourings such as soy beans, garlic, chilies and sugar. It is an essential seasoning, dipping sauce and spread in Chinese cooking, popular with moo shu pork and Peking duck.

Japanese gelatin (Kanten) An agar-like substance made from tengusa seaweed. It is the primary ingredient for jelly-like desserts.

Kaofu A sponge-like steamed loaf made with wheat flour, baking powder and gluten. Like seitan, a wheat gluten product made by washing wheat flour dough with water until all the starch dissolves, it has a mild grainy taste, but kaofu is moister and readily absorbs flavours. It is available fresh, frozen or canned and is used as a meat replacement.

Kecap manis A thick, syrupy Indonesian soy sauce that is sweetened with palm sugar and has a more complex flavour than regular soy sauce. It is used as a seasoning.

Kimchi (Kimchee) A traditional Korean dish made by fermenting napa cabbage in brined vinegar, garlic and red chilies. Variations made with other cabbages or with daikon also exist, as does an unfermented Japanese version of kimchi. It can be a main dish, a side dish, a condiment or an ingredient in other dishes.

Kombu (Konbu) An edible kelp that is sun-dried to produce thick rubber-like sheets that soften when boiled. Charcoal black with an umami flavour, kombu is combined with water and bonito flakes to make the Japanese dashi soup stock.

Mei gui lu cooking wine A distilled Chinese white wine made with rose petals and rock sugar, said to have a medicinal effect. Salt is added to the cooking wine version. It is commonly used in Chinese cooking, especially with poultry dishes.

Mirin A sweet Japanese rice wine similar to sake but with less alcohol. It is commonly used for cooking and seasoning.

Miso A traditional Japanese seasoning paste made from fermented soy beans, rice or barley with salt and fungus and used to flavour sauces and soups. The most popular variations are *shiro* (white) miso made mainly from rice and barley and *aka* (red) miso made mainly from steamed soy beans and aged for a long time.

Nam prik (Nam phrik) A red Thai chili paste made by crushing chilies with garlic and shrimp paste in a mortar and pestle. Regional variations may include fish sauce, tamarind pulp and/or dried fish. It is a condiment and a dipping sauce.

Noodles, Chinese Long thin strands made from wheat flour, rice flour or mung bean starch plus salt and water and dried, boiled or fried. Fresh ones are now available in Asian markets and noodle shops. Popular varieties include *egg noodles,* used in dishes like chow mein; *cellophane noodles,* which are skinny, lightweight and translucent threads made from potato starch or green mung beans and have an elastic texture when cooked, *hor fan noodles,* which are broad, snow-white noodles made from rice flour, and *rice vermicelli,* which are thin white noodles made from rice flour.

Noodles, Japanese Long, thin strands made from buckwheat flour, wheat flour or agar. Among the most popular varieties are *ramen*, round yellow noodles made from wheat flour and often deep-fried and served in soup. They can be fresh or dried, especially as instant noodles. *Soba* are Japanese buckwheat noodles used in salads; *somen* are thin, white Japanese noodles made from wheat flour and usually served cold; and *udon* are thick, round noodles made with wheat or corn flour and often served in soup.

Nori An edible seaweed that is shredded, dried on racks and pressed into paper-thin dark-green or black sheets. Slightly salty, it is used to wrap sushi, flavour soups and garnish many Japanese dishes.

Oyster sauce A thick, brown sauce made by condensing oyster extracts, which are obtained by boiling the shellfish in water so that they release their white broth. The authentic sauce is expensive to produce, so most versions combine oyster extracts with sugar, salt, water, cornstarch and colour. It is a savoury flavouring for stir fries, meat and vegetable dishes.

Palm sugar (Coconut sugar, Arenga sugar) Extracted from the sap of palm trees, it looks like regular brown sugar but has a purer, longer-lasting sweetness. It is used in cooking, baking and beverages.

Paneer (Panir) A fresh, white, unripened Indian cheese made from whole cow's or buffalo's milk and curdled with lemon or lime juice. It is generally unsalted and can be added to sweet or savoury dishes.

Panko Crisp, airy Japanese bread crumbs made from crustless bread. It is used as a coating for deep-fried foods.

Pickled ginger (Gari, Sushi ginger) Thinly sliced young ginger marinated in sweet vinegar. In Japan, natural-coloured pickled ginger is known as *amazu shoga* and cleanses the palate between different types of sushi. *Beni shoga* is ginger that has been cut into thin strips, coloured red and preserved by pickling. It is used as a garnish or a condiment for savoury dishes, especially noodles.

Pidan (Hundred-year eggs, Century eggs, thousand-year eggs) Raw duck eggs preserved in a mixture of lime, ashes and salt for 35 to 45 days until the egg white is firm and charcoal coloured and the yolk is dark green. The mildly truffle-flavoured eggs are used in congee, and sliced pidan mixed with pickled ginger is a delicacy in certain regions.

Plum sauce A light-brown condiment made with plums, apricots, sugar, vinegar and a hint of chili pepper. It is sweet-sour and served with spring rolls and Chinese barbecued duck.

Ponzu sauce A light yellow Japanese condiment made by simmering rice vinegar and/or lemon juice, mirin and/or sake, kombu and dried bonito flakes and then adding the juice of one or more citrus fruits. It can also be mixed with soy sauce (shoyu) and used as a dipping sauce.

Rice The milled seeds of the rice plant are commonly steamed or boiled as an accompaniment to many Asian meals. Among the most common kinds are *brown rice,* which has been milled to remove the outer husk and has a nutty flavour and a chewy texture; *white rice (short- or long-grain),* which has been further milled to remove the remaining husk and the germ and has a less pronounced flavour; *basmati rice,* a long-grain Indian rice with a firmer, drier texture and very aromatic, slightly nutty flavour; *glutinous rice (sweet rice, sticky rice),* a rounder short-grain variety with a chewier texture and that can be white, pinkish red or black; *jasmine rice,* an aromatic long-grain Thai white rice; *black rice,* a chewy, perky long-grain rice used mostly for desserts.

Rice paper wrappers (Vietnamese rice paper) Thin, round, paper-like sheets made from the pith of a rice paper plant native to Taiwan and used to wrap salad rolls and pastry rolls. Moisten them with water or wrap them in a damp tea towel before using them to prevent them from cracking.

Rice vinegar, Chinese Vinegar made from fermented rice and used for cooking. *White rice vinegar* is colourless and made from regular rice. It is less acidic and milder than regular distilled white vinegar. *Red rice vinegar* is stronger tasting and reddish coloured because it is made from red yeast rice. *Black rice vinegar* is darker and smokier and is usually made from black glutinous rice, but millet or sorghum may be used, too.

Rice vinegar, Japanese A colourless, mild-flavoured vinegar made from fermented rice or sake lees and used for cooking. *Seasoned rice vinegar,* which is added to cooked rice to make sushi, is Japanese rice vinegar plus sake (or mirin), salt and sugar.

Rock sugar, Chinese (Bing tang) Yellow lumps of crystallized sugar made from refined cane sugar and used mostly for cooking, especially in making desserts.

Sago A starch extracted from the sago (and other tropical) palms that is processed into flour, meal and sago pearls, which are similar to tapioca and commonly used in Taiwanese bubble teas. The small, dry, opaque balls should be soaked or cooked.

SHOWN HERE: *Dried banana flowers, rock sugar, whole banana flowers, ginger, garlic, black peppercorns and star anise.*

Sake A Japanese rice wine made from specially selected rice that is steamed and fermented. There are many varieties with differing flavours and degrees of dryness or sweetness. For sipping, sake can be enjoyed cold or hot.

Sambal A chili-based condiment. Spicy Indonesian *sambal oelek* is a bright red paste made by crushing chilies with salt and brown sugar. *Sambal kecap manis* is a sweeter variation.

Seitan See Kaofu.

Sesame paste (Tahini) Originally from China, this condiment is made from toasted, ground sesame seeds and has a similar flavour and texture to peanut butter.

Shaoxing wine (Huadiu) A traditional Huangjiu rice wine from the Shaoxing region of China and made from fermented rice. Reddish in colour, it is not distilled and has a lower alcohol content than many rice wines. As salt has been added, use it only in cooking.

Shrimp paste (Bagoong, Terasi) A thick greyish-pink to purple paste made from fermented ground shrimp that is dried, formed into sauces or blocks and used as a seasoning. It has a pungent smell and an intense fishy, nutty flavour.

Soy sauce (Shoyu, Jiang yu) A light brown to dark salty sauce made from boiled and fermented soy beans and roasted wheat or barley. Variations include *dark soy sauce,* a thicker sauce sweetened with molasses; *light soy sauce,* a thinner, opaque brown liquid with a saltier flavour than regular soy sauce; *low-sodium soy sauce,* a thin soy sauce with less salt than regular soy sauce; *mushroom soy sauce,* a dark soy sauce enhanced with mushroom essence; *soy paste,* a paste-like dark soy sauce thickened with starch and sugar; and *tamari,* a wheat-free Japanese soy sauce that is thicker and darker than regular soy sauce.

Tapioca A starch extracted from the root of the cassava plant that can be dried and ground into flour or formed into pearls of various sizes. The pearls must be soaked before cooking and are popular for desserts and bubble tea. Tapioca flour is used as a thickening agent and in gluten-free baking.

Tempeh (Tempe) A firm, savoury Indonesian cake made with fermented soy beans and used as a meat replacement. It is chewy and dense with a nutty flavour, and it is often marinated. Once cooked, it can be crumbled, sautéed, stir-fried and added to soups, sandwiches and stews or used as a condiment or a side dish.

Wakame A dark-green, slightly sweet edible seaweed used to flavour soups and salads. It is sold in dried or salted leaves that expand and become slippery when added to liquid.

Wasabi (Japanese horseradish, Wasabe) A strong-tasting, light-green condiment made from the root of a wild Japanese plant that belongs to the horseradish family. It is grated fresh or dried and ground into a powder mixed with water to form a paste, which is a popular complement to sushi.

Won ton skins (Won ton wrappers, Spring roll wrappers) Paper-thin round or square sheets of flour mixed with eggs and water used to wrap won tons, spring rolls and other dim sum items. They are available as white Shanghai wrappers (fluffier) and yellow Cantonese wrappers (with a touch of lye). Bring them to room temperature before filling them and keep them moist with a damp towel while working with them.

XO sauce The highest grade of chili oil, this fiery hot condiment is made with chili flakes, chili sauce, garlic, shallots, dried scallops and dried shrimp. It is added to savoury dishes to enhance their flavour.

1. **Asian service** Asian meals are enjoyed communally, whether at home or in restaurants. Large platters of food are placed in the middle of the table for sharing all at once, and diners reach across to take what they want from any dish at any time. Occasionally, for special occasions or banquets, individual courses are served in a specific order.

   Most cooks try to create a balance of dishes. Typically, a meal may include vegetable dishes, meat dishes, seafood dishes and/or combination dishes. Also important is a range of flavours, textures and temperatures. There are also one-dish meals such as noodle soups, chow mein, udon, donburi (Japanese rice bowl) and stir-fried rice that are served as quick lunch items.

2. **Dietary preferences** Religion plays an important part in the dietary preferences of many Asians. Muslims don't eat pork, some Buddhists don't eat any animal products and avoid the "pungent spices" in the garlic, leek and onion family, and some Hindus don't eat beef or garlic and onions. Many Asians also abstain from meats or other foods for health or other reasons. Adapt any of these dishes to suit your own dietary preferences, such as using tofu, kaofu, seitan, tempeh and/or grains in place of meat or substituting seafood for pork or making dishes with spices instead of garlic and onions. You can also make a delicious aromatic-free soup stock from rinsed and rehydrated Chinese black mushrooms, soy bean sprouts and corn.

   If possible, reserve one board for meat and seafood, another for roots and vegetables. Otherwise, use the front of the board for meat and the back for vegetables. Clean cutting boards with a mild detergent and warm water, rinse them well and towel dry them before and after use. Some Asians also maintain a separate board for cutting cooked foods. Thick wooden boards are most popular, but bamboo and plastic ones are fine, too.

3. Timing Serving all your dishes at once requires planning. Start the braised and stewed dishes well ahead of time. Steam the rice while you're making the quick-cooking recipes. For stir-fried, pan-fried or grilled dishes, have all your ingredients ready to go before you begin so that you can add them immediately, to keep everything fresh, hot and properly cooked. Set up your work area so that the seasonings, sauces and spices are close at hand.

4. Drinks and beverages Typically, meals are accompanied by cups of hot tea or cold water; however, Taiwanese bubble tea is meant as a snack rather than a drink served with food. Beer is the most popular alcoholic beverage in Asia, and you can serve it cold with many meals. In social situations, drinking distilled Chinese rice wine with a high alcohol content (50% or more) is popular in China; in Japan, many people sip sake, hot or cold, with their meal. Increasingly, Asians are drinking cocktails, wine, Scotch and brandy with their food, so feel free to do the same.

5. Rice, bread and buns Throughout Asia, rice is the staple grain. Most people eat steamed long-grain rice, including jasmine rice, as an accompaniment to the meal, though in India, firmer, more fragrant basmati rice is favoured, and in Japan, short-grain rice, which is more glutinous, is preferred. Most Asians have traditionally eaten white rice, but brown and wild rice are now making their way into restaurants and households, especially in North America. Large bowls of plain, steamed rice are served on the side, family-style, with every meal.

Rice can easily be prepared on the stovetop, but most Asians use an electric rice cooker. If you're not sure about the appropriate ratio of water to rice, the rice cooker contains markings that make this step easy. Add a few drops of freshly squeezed lemon juice to the pot of uncooked rice and water for fluffier and more fragrant rice.

Breads and steamed buns are also an integral part of some meals. Like rice, they are served communally so diners can help themselves, and it's not uncommon to find rice and bread at the same meal. In India, breads are commonly served to soak up rich curries. In China and other parts of Asia, steamed buns and breads typically accompany saucy dishes.

6. **Sauces and condiments** Just as salt, pepper and ketchup are served with many meals in North America, Asian cooks offer staple sauces and condiments to enhance the flavour of their meals. Serve sambals with Indonesian meals, XO sauce with Chinese dishes, soy sauce with Japanese food, chutneys with Indian curries, kimchi and other such small dishes of cold or room-temperature food (called *banchan*) with Korean meals. Refrigerate all store-bought sauces in airtight containers.

7. **Oils** Many Asian dishes are cooked over direct heat rather than in an oven, so the most common methods are searing, pan-frying, stir-frying, deep-frying, blanching, roasting and grilling. Consequently, Asians use a fair amount of oil in their dishes, to prevent foods from sticking and to bring out their flavour. Canola oil is preferred, but peanut oil and corn oil are common, too. Butter is rarely used, though ghee (clarified butter) is popular in India. Unless a recipe specifically says to start cooking in cold oil, heat it first before you add any other ingredients! The hot, sizzling oil cures the food, preserves its texture and imparts "wok energy," an umami flavour derived by cooking food in a red-hot wok.

For a crispy texture when pan-frying, use a small amount of oil. When deep-frying, use enough oil to just cover the ingredients and cook them in batches. You can filter and reuse frying oil, but when you're done with it, allow it to cool completely, transfer it to a disposable container and discard it in the garbage or at a recycling facility (never pour hot oil down the drain).

8. **Spice mixtures** For best results, buy the best, freshest spices you can to make these dishes. You can buy whole spices and roast and grind them yourself (do this in batches and store leftovers) or buy premade mixtures. Store ground or whole dry spices in an airtight container in a cool, dark place for up to 6 months. Be sure to label them with the name and date. Place leftover spice pastes in an airtight container and refrigerate for up to 7 days. Drizzling a thin layer of oil over the paste before covering it will prolong its shelf life by another week.

9. **Leftovers** Most Asians make their food fresh for each meal and consume it immediately or at least the next day. If there's too much food, invite more people to join the meal! Most of these dishes are not designed to be made ahead, refrigerated or frozen; however, you can certainly keep leftovers in an airtight container in the refrigerator for a couple of days. Some delicate ingredients, such as bean sprouts or deep-fried foods, may become soggy, and starchy ingredients, such as noodles, rice, breads and buns may become tough. Having said that, some dishes, like stews and curries, taste even better the next day, once the seasoning and spices have had a chance to mingle.

At the end of the meal, loosen and fluff any unused cooked rice left in the rice cooker or pot to prevent it from setting into a starchy mass. Reheated rice loses some of its original taste and texture, so many Chinese refrigerate it in an airtight container and then use it to make fried rice or congee. Other options, though less traditional, are to add it to soups or stews or to make rice pudding. Freezing rice is not recommended, because it loses its fluffiness when thawed.

STEAMING BOWLS of aromatic soup are not only delicious and nourishing, but many Asian versions also have medicinal properties. They can be cloudy or clear, hot or warm, light or hearty. Long-boiled Chinese herbal soups made with specific quantities of meats, roots, vegetables, herbs and dried fruits can prepare the body for seasonal and climatic adjustments, prevent disease, fight allergies, cleanse and rebalance the inner body. Some broths warm and strengthen the body during the cold seasons, whereas others cool and soothe in the hot, humid months. Try the wholesome Tilapia, Daikon and Pepper Soup, the warming Spiced Kimchi Casserole Soup or the comforting Vietnamese Beef Pho'. Except in India, soups are usually thickened by adding a paste of water and starch rather than cream or milk.

Serve these soups Asian-style by presenting them in a large pot in the middle of the table so that guests can serve themselves. Or ladle them into individual bowls to accompany steamed rice. Thick or thin, soups are eaten with a spoon in India, Thailand, Korea and China, but it's common in Japan to bring the bowl to your mouth and drink from it. Consider this permission to slurp any of these broths or noodle soups at home!

SOUPS

NO-FIN SHARK FIN SOUP

Serves 2

1 pkg (200 g) fresh
enoki mushrooms

2 Tbsp vegetable oil

10 Szechuan peppercorns

1 Tbsp minced ginger

1 Tbsp shredded Chinese
onions (or green onions)

1 Tbsp Shaoxing rice wine

1 Tbsp dark soy sauce

¼ tsp white sugar

1 cup chicken stock

1 tsp potato starch

SHARK-FIN SOUP is an expensive and controversial delicacy usually served on special occasions. The authentic traditional versions are made with chicken and Chinese ham that's been simmered for a long time to create a delicious, salty broth. Here, Chef Zhou, who is originally from Beijing but trained both there and in Vancouver, gives this dish a West Coast twist. Substitute regular green onions when Chinese onions (king onions) are out of season.

TRIM AND DISCARD 1½ inches from bottom of mushrooms and separate by hand.

In a small pot, bring 2 cups water to a boil on high heat. Blanch mushrooms for 30 seconds to the remove raw fungus odour. Drain in a colander and set aside.

To the pot, add 1 Tbsp of the vegetable oil and heat on medium-high. Add peppercorns and brown for 90 seconds, or until they become dark. Drain oil into a small bowl and set aside. Discard peppercorns.

In a medium saucepan, heat remaining 1 Tbsp vegetable oil on medium-high. Add ginger and green onions and sauté for 2 to 3 minutes, or until golden brown. Slowly add wine, soy sauce, sugar and chicken stock and bring to a boil, then reduce the heat to medium.

In a small bowl, mix potato starch with 2 Tbsp cold water. Pour the mixture into the saucepan and stir gently for 15 to 20 seconds or until soup thickens. Add mushrooms and cook for 15 to 20 seconds. Divide soup among 2 large bowls. Drizzle with peppercorn oil and serve hot.

TILAPIA, DAIKON AND PEPPER SOUP

Serves 4

1 tsp sea salt	6 slices ginger, skin on	1 red bell pepper, in ½- × 2-inch strips
½ tsp ground white pepper + more to taste	2 whole green onions	1 yellow bell pepper, in ½- × 2-inch strips
1 live tilapia, 14 to 16 oz, scaled, cleaned and patted dry	1 Tbsp Shaoxing rice wine	
1 Tbsp vegetable oil	10 oz daikon, peeled and cut in ½- × 2-inch strips	

SPRINKLE ½ TSP of the sea salt and ground white pepper on both sides of the tilapia. Set aside for 15 minutes.

In a wok, heat vegetable oil on high for 15 seconds. Using a spatula, gently slide tilapia into the wok, reduce the heat to medium and brown for 3 minutes. Carefully turn tilapia over and brown for another 3 minutes. Add ginger, green onion, wine and daikon and cook for 15 seconds. Slowly pour in 6 cups water, bring to a full boil on high heat and allow to boil, partially covered, on medium-high heat for 30 minutes. The soup should begin to turn milky.

Reduce the heat to medium-low, cover and cook for 10 minutes. Increase the heat to high, bring soup to a full boil again and add bell peppers. Cook for another 2 to 3 minutes, uncovered. Season with the remaining ½ tsp salt and pepper to taste. Use a large slotted spoon or ladle to transfer the fish to a platter. Ladle soup into bowls and serve hot.

Refrigerate leftover soup in an airtight container for up to 1 day.

ALTHOUGH CANTONESE enjoy making long-boiled soups *(lo for tong)*, simmered for hours with specific ingredients chosen for their health benefits, quick-boiled soups made with fresh and seasonal ingredients are more common in other provinces. This easy-to-make, quick-boiled soup is a good example of just how simple and delicious Chinese soups can be. Tilapia is now a top choice for Asian cooks because it is available year-round, has a meaty texture and is environmentally sustainable.

Chef Liu is the Group Executive Chef of Kirin's five award-winning restaurants. This recipe, which is featured at the chain's original location, Kirin Mandarin (Kirin Downtown), combines traditional Mandarin techniques and flavours with a local twist.

Using the whole fish, and browning it first to keep it intact during the boiling process, renders a cream-like colour and texture. Before serving the soup, remove the fish, which can be eaten separately, with a small bowl of light soy sauce for dipping.

WATERMELON AND DUNGENESS CRAB SOUP

Serves 8

2 stalks fresh lemon grass

2 Tbsp grapeseed oil

4 kaffir lime leaves, julienned

3 Tbsp finely minced shallots

2 Tbsp finely minced young ginger

2 Tbsp finely chopped garlic

1 to 2 small hot Thai chili peppers with seeds, finely minced

8 cups fresh seedless watermelon, in 1-inch dice

2 Tbsp fresh kaffir lime juice

1 cup coconut cream (not milk)

3 Tbsp fish sauce

½ lb fresh Dungeness crabmeat, picked over for cartilage

¼ cup finely chopped fresh cilantro

¼ cup finely chopped fresh Thai basil

1 fresh kaffir lime, in 8 slices, or 8 whole Thai chili peppers (optional)

EDIBLE CANADA at the Market is a new restaurant at Granville Island's Public Market from the founder of Edible BC. It showcases the best of local B.C. and Canadian ingredients and international flavours. This Thai-inspired soup combines fresh B.C. Dungeness crab with coconut, lemon grass, kaffir lime and fiery chilies for a refreshing new Pacific Northwest summer classic. Be sure to use young ginger, which is juicy and fleshy with very little fibre. Serve this soup hot or cold, on its own or with slices of fresh bread. This soup does not keep well.

USING A SHARP knife, cut each lemon grass stalk 3 to 4 inches from the bottom, where the light and green portions meet. Peel and discard the top layer of the light part of each stalk, revealing the tender, white inner hearts. Slice these and mince them finely. (Reserve the remaining green leaves to use in other dishes.)

Heat a large stockpot on medium and add grapeseed oil. Add lemon grass, lime leaves, shallots, ginger, garlic and minced chilies and sauté until fragrant and wilted, 2 to 3 minutes. Do not brown, or the soup will have a toasted flavour. Stir in watermelon, reduce the heat to medium-low and simmer for about 20 minutes until the fruit has mostly broken apart. Remove from the heat, allow to cool slightly, then, using a hand-held blender, purée the watermelon mixture.

Place a fine-mesh sieve over a large, clean bowl. Strain soup into the bowl, discarding any solids, then return to the pot. Add lime juice, coconut cream and 2 Tbsp of the fish sauce to the pot and stir well. To serve soup warm, increase the heat to medium and reheat for 1 to 2 minutes, stirring constantly. (For chilled soup, ladle soup into 8 large bowls and refrigerate uncovered for about 2 hours.)

Just before serving, combine crabmeat, cilantro, Thai basil and the remaining 1 Tbsp fish sauce in a small bowl and toss lightly. Divide crabmeat evenly among 8 soup bowls, piling it high in the centre, then pour soup around the crab. Garnish each serving with a slice of lime or a whole chili pepper.

THAI CHICKEN AND COCONUT MILK SOUP

Serves 2

2 cups chicken stock

1 cup coconut milk

4 kaffir lime leaves, halved

½ stalk lemon grass, in 4 pieces

1 oz galangal, in 5 slices

8 oz raw white or dark chicken meat, sliced

¼ cup sliced white crimini mushrooms

3 Tbsp fish sauce

1½ Tbsp white sugar

½ Tbsp Thai chili paste (nam prik)

2 ½ Tbsp fresh lime juice

1 tsp chopped fresh cilantro

1 tsp chopped green onions, white and green parts

COCONUT IS by far the most-used tropical fruit in Southeast Asian cooking. Whether used for its milk or its meat, coconut adds a mild sweetness and smoothness to many beverages and dishes. Coconut milk, coconut cream and coconut juice are readily available in Asian food stores in cans, jars or cartons.

IN A MEDIUM pot, combine chicken stock and coconut milk on medium-high heat. Add lime leaves, lemon grass and galangal and bring to a boil. Gently stir in chicken, mushrooms, fish sauce, sugar and chili paste and bring back to the boil. Cook for 3 to 4 minutes or until chicken is cooked through. Turn off the heat. Stir in lime juice. Transfer soup to a large tureen and garnish with cilantro and green onions. Serve hot.

PINE MUSHROOM AND SHRIMP SOUP

Serves 4

2 tsp sake

one 1½-inch square kombu

3 Tbsp shaved dry bonito flakes

½ tsp salt

½ tsp light soy sauce
(not low-sodium)

½ tsp mirin

4 oz hand-peeled cooked shrimp

8 pine mushrooms, in ⅛-inch slices

1 tsp dried wakame seaweed

1 Tbsp chopped green onions,
white and green parts

1 Tbsp chopped mitsuba (optional)

LIGHTLY MOISTEN the corner of a clean cloth with 1 tsp of the sake. Thoroughly wipe kombu to remove the fine powder on its surface. In a small stockpot, combine kombu and 2 cups water and cook on medium-high heat for 4 to 5 minutes. Before water comes to a boil, turn off the heat and remove and discard the kombu. Add bonito flakes and allow to steep for 30 minutes. Place a fine-mesh sieve over a small bowl. Strain broth, discarding bonito flakes and any other solids. This broth is called dashi.

Return dashi to the stockpot and heat on medium-high. Add salt, soy sauce, mirin and the remaining 1 tsp sake, bring to a gentle boil and immediately reduce the heat to low. Add shrimp, mushrooms and wakame and turn off the heat.

Ladle the soup evenly into 4 soup bowls. Garnish each serving with green onions and mitsuba and serve hot.

Refrigerate leftover soup in an airtight container for up to 1 day.

EARTHY, AROMATIC matsutake (pine) mushrooms are the essence of this soothing, hot soup. Whereas the pine mushrooms grown in Asia are mostly brownish, the Pacific Northwest is home to white matsutakes, which can be found at farmers' markets and specialty grocery stores when they are in season, from August to November. For Japanese ingredients, such as kombu and wakame seaweeds, bonito flakes (known as *katsuobushi* in Japanese) and mirin cooking wine, visit Japanese or other Asian supermarkets.

BEEF PHO'

Serves 4

PHO' STOCK

2 large onions, in ¼-inch slices	2 beef leg bones	¼ cup whole star anise
8 thick slices ginger, skin on, smashed	4 lbs beef back bones	¼ cup Szechuan peppercorns
	3 lbs beef briskets, in 3 equal slabs	4 cinnamon sticks, crushed
		20 to 25 whole fresh nutmegs

PHO' IS synonymous with Vietnamese cuisine. Steaming hot and loaded with meat, bean sprouts and fresh basil leaves, it is undoubtedly comfort food. The secret to a great bowl of pho' is the stock. Whether chicken or beef, the soup stock must be simmered for hours to bring out the rich flavour of the meat and the bones. This recipe comes from Chef Ha, who has been making and serving pho' in Metro Vancouver for more than 30 years. In the mid-1980s, she opened Happy Garden Restaurant on Westminster Highway, the first restaurant in Richmond to serve authentic Vietnamese fare. At New Asia Deli, she offers Hong Kong street food and Taiwanese bubble tea as well.

Making a perfect pot of beef pho' stock at home is a task, so allow lots of time, and be patient! You'll need a huge stockpot, at least 36 quarts, to allow the stock to boil down. Pho' should be consumed the instant it's assembled so that the rising steam can deliver the aroma of the soup and the toppings and so that the noodles don't soak any longer than necessary.

PHO' STOCK Preheat a toaster oven to 350°F. Arrange onions and ginger on a rack and bake for 10 minutes. Set aside.

Half-fill a 10- to 12-qt stockpot with water and bring to a boil on high heat. Add leg and back bones and briskets and blanch for 15 minutes. Drain and discard water.

Make a spice sachet by placing a 10-inch square piece of cheesecloth on a clean work surface. Arrange star anise, peppercorns, cinnamon and nutmegs in the middle of the cheesecloth. Gather the corners of the cheesecloth, completely encasing the spices, and tie tightly with a piece of kitchen twine. You can also use fish bags or herb bags in place of the cheesecloth. They come in two sizes (10 × 12 inches or 8 × 10 inches) and are available in Asian markets.

Place the 36-qt stockpot on the stove, fill it ¾ full with water and add onions, ginger, bones and briskets and the spice sachet. Bring to a boil on high heat and cook, uncovered, for 3 hours. Reduce the heat to medium and cook, partially covered, for 4 more hours. Reduce the heat to low and simmer, covered, for a further 4 hours. Turn off the heat and set the pot, covered, in a cool place (ideally outside or on a covered patio) overnight.

Using a spoon, skim off and discard the fat on the surface of the stock. Bring stock to a boil on high heat, then remove the lid and cook for 2 hours. Reduce the heat to low and cook for 4 hours, partially covered. Cover the pot, remove from the heat and allow it to cool (outside or on the patio) for 2 to 3 hours.

Using a spoon, skim off and discard the fat on the surface of the stock. Using a slotted spoon, skim off onions and ginger; with a pair of tongs, remove meat, bones

PHO'

4 to 5 qts beef pho' stock	2 fresh red hot chili peppers, sliced (optional)	4 to 6 oz raw beef tenderloin, thinly sliced
½ tsp salt	1 fresh lime, in 8 pieces	2 green onions, white and green parts, shredded or diced
1 Tbsp fish sauce	1 Tbsp sriracha chili sauce	1 small onion, julienned
2 cups bean sprouts	1 Tbsp hoisin sauce	
2 bunches fresh Thai basil	2 pkgs (each 16 oz) Vietnamese dried vermicelli (rice stick), soaked in water for 1 hour	
1 bunch fresh cilantro, coarsely chopped		

and spice sachet. Allow to rest for another hour, then skim off the fat on the surface one more time. Strain the broth through a fine-mesh sieve to remove any residue. You should have 8 to 10 quarts of stock. Freshly made stock can be stored in the pot for up to 2 days. Bring it to a boil before leaving it overnight, then reboil it again just before serving.

PHO' About 30 minutes before you plan to make the pho', bring stock to a boil on high heat. Reduce the heat to medium and allow to boil while assembling the pho'.

In a medium saucepan, bring 8 cups water to a boil on high heat. Stir in salt and fish sauce. Add bean sprouts and blanch for 1 minute. Using a slotted spoon, transfer bean sprouts to a plate and set aside. Reduce the heat to low and allow the broth to simmer.

Bring pho' stock to a full boil on high heat. While the pho' is heating, arrange basil, cilantro, chilies and lime on 4 individual plates. Pour sriracha and hoisin sauce into 2 dipping bowls. Arrange these condiments and the plate of bean sprouts in the middle of the table so that guests can help themselves.

Return the broth to a boil on high heat. Using a fine-mesh metal strainer, blanch 2 handfuls of vermicelli for 30 seconds and place them in a soup bowl. Top with a quarter of the sliced beef, a quarter of the green onions and a quarter of the onions. Ladle in enough stock to just cover the contents of the bowl. Repeat with the remaining noodles, beef, green onions and onions and serve. Guests can add whichever combination of condiments they prefer while the stock is still steaming hot.

SPICED KIMCHI CASSEROLE SOUP

Serves 4

2 tsp butter

2 tsp sesame oil

4 tsp Korean red chili powder

½ lb pork belly, in ¼-inch slices

2 tsp minced ginger

2 Tbsp white wine

½ tsp freshly ground white pepper

1 cup kimchi, in 2-inch pieces

½ onion, sliced

2 cups beef stock

1 cup rice water (water used to rinse the rice before cooking)

1 tsp sea salt

2 tsp white sugar

2 tsp corn syrup

2 tsp soy sauce

4 oz firm tofu, in ¼- × 1-inch pieces

1 to 4 green onions, white and green parts, in 2-inch lengths

CELADON IS located in the Hilton in Whistler, so if you're craving some heat and some authentic Korean cuisine or modern Asian food after a day on the slopes, you can get your fill here. The "casserole" in this recipe refers to the dish it's served in and it's one hot pot of steaming and spicy soup that will drive away any winter chills. Go easy with the Korean chili paste, which adds serious heat to the already very spicy soup. Start with a tiny amount and add more, to taste. (Keep leftover chili paste in an airtight container for up to 2 days.) Serve this soup with rice both so that you have rice water and so that you can sop up the juices and temper the fire.

IN A SMALL saucepan, heat butter and sesame oil on medium, add chili powder, mix well and set aside. This is your very hot Korean chili paste.

Heat a heavy, deep-sided sauté pan or a heat-resistant casserole (if you don't have a casserole, use a heavy pot) on medium-high. Add pork belly and cook until crispy, 5 to 7 minutes. Add ginger, wine and white pepper and sauté for 1 minute, then add kimchi and onions and sauté for 2 minutes more. Slowly pour in beef stock, 1 cup water and rice water, then stir in sea salt, sugar, corn syrup and soy sauce and bring to a moderate boil for 15 to 20 minutes. Add tofu and green onions, just before serving. Stir in ½ tsp chili paste. Place the remaining chili paste in a small bowl. As guests help themselves to soup, pass the bowl of chili paste so they can add more as desired. Refrigerate leftover soup in an airtight container for up to 2 days.

HASTINGS STREET IS the only road that runs in a straight line across Vancouver. From its start at the waterfront in the West End of Vancouver to its terminus at the foot of Simon Fraser University in Burnaby, it's packed with strip malls and industrial blocks housing many shops and restaurants that don't look like anything special but serve good, inexpensive food in comfortable surroundings.

Originally, the section between Gore and Main on the edge of Chinatown had a pronounced Chinese character and even spilled farther east about two decades ago. On Lok Restaurant, the longest-standing Chinese restaurant on Hastings, is a holdover from that era of good-and-cheap-style neighbourhood eateries. Its menu is still completely unpretentious, its portions large and freshly made and its prices very reasonable. Try the rice with three barbecued meats. Likewise, Koko Japanese Restaurant has been in the same location just down from On Lok for about 25 years and continues to offer great value, quality and taste, especially with its bento lunch box.

Just a few blocks east, Viet Thanh Market marks the beginning of the strip decorated by famed Asian restaurants. Seri Malaysia Restaurant, known for authentic and homestyle food—especially delicious roti, has been around for years. Bo Laksa King's Bubbles and Bits offers inviting Southeast Asian cuisine and modern drinks and snacks; Luda serves classic and innovative southern Chinese cuisine, including highly recommended hot pot dishes. Along with Japanese sushi and sashimi houses, izakaya-style bistros, Chinese dim sum and seafood restaurants and pho' noodle houses, these ten blocks between Nanaimo and Rupert have restored Hasting Street's pan-Asian accent.

Now a truly multi-ethnic neighbourhood, this area is popular with locals. By day, young homemakers with kids might duck into a coffeehouse, then pick up groceries at the Asian market and the continental deli. Teenagers might buy a bubble tea or grab a burger from the nearest fast-food outlet. And office workers are as likely to eat lunch in a sushi bar as they are to go a few doors down for a plate of pasta. In the evening, however, it's loyal customers from across the city looking for parking spots in front of their favourite restaurants that keep this section of Hastings alive!

PORK, DRIED SCALLOP AND PIDAN CONGEE

Serves 6 to 8

1½ lbs lean pork, in ¹⁄₁₆-inch slices

1 tsp salt

6 to 8 small to medium dried scallops

1½ cups long-grain rice (or more if you prefer thicker congee), rinsed and drained

4 pidan, peeled and cut in ½-inch dice

Ground white pepper to taste

¼ cup chopped green onions, white and green parts

¼ cup chopped fresh cilantro

STEAMING HOT and often enjoyed with an array of condiments, congee is the ultimate Cantonese comfort food. It reminds many Chinese of the Sunday morning family brunch prepared by Mom or Grandma. Congee can be plain or cooked with vegetables or with meat or seafood. Brined, sun-dried scallops have a subtle sweet flavour and are the foremost taste enhancer for premium soup stocks and congee. *Pidan* is the Mandarin phonic transliteration for preserved eggs known as thousand-year eggs, which are available in most Chinese grocery stores and Asian supermarkets.

Sun Fresh Bakery is a Chinatown institution. Located on Keefer Street, it's known for its steamed buns, dumplings, rice rolls and this famous pidan congee, which is neither too thick nor too thin. Congee is meant to be eaten as soon as it's cooked, because it becomes glutinous the longer it sits.

IN A MEDIUM bowl, toss pork and salt together, cover and set aside for 2 hours.

Rinse scallops with water and place them in a small bowl. Add ¾ cup water and allow to soak for 2 hours. Reserve the soaking water.

Fill a 12-qt pot ¾ full of water, add rice, scallops and their soaking water, and pidan, cover and bring to a boil on high heat. Remove the lid and cook, uncovered, for about 1 hour.

Reduce the heat to medium-low, cover and simmer for 10 minutes, stirring once or twice to prevent rice from sticking. This step settles the congee, allowing the rice and liquid to meld.

Increase the heat to high again and bring congee back to a boil. Add pork, and, using a whisk, break up any clumps of meat. Cook, uncovered, for 15 to 20 minutes.

Reduce the heat to low, cover and simmer for another 10 minutes until congee has the consistency of porridge. Season to taste with salt and freshly ground white pepper. Arrange green onions and cilantro in 2 small bowls and serve on the side as condiments. Ladle congee into individual bowls and serve hot.

SPINACH PANEER SOUP

Serves 4

3 cups chopped fresh spinach	1 tsp ground cumin	8 to 10 oz paneer, in 1-inch cubes
1 cup chopped cucumber, unpeeled	½ tsp ground coriander	2 Tbsp fresh lemon juice
1 Tbsp butter	1 tsp ginger paste (or finely minced ginger)	1 cup plain Greek yogurt
1 tsp freshly ground black pepper		

IN A MEDIUM saucepan, combine spinach, cucumber and 3½ cups water and cook on medium heat until vegetables are tender, about 6 minutes. Set aside and allow to cool for 20 minutes. Transfer to a blender and purée until you have a paste.

Place the saucepan on high heat, add butter, black pepper, cumin, coriander, ginger and paneer and stir well. Season with salt to taste. Gently pour in the spinach-cucumber paste, stirring gently. Reduce the heat to medium, add lemon juice, stir gently for 30 seconds and cook for 5 to 7 minutes. Ladle soup into individual bowls and serve hot, topped with a dollop of yogurt.

MOST INDIAN soups are vegetarian and are considered healthy, comfort food. This easy soup is from Curry 2 U, an Indian fast-food restaurant on Granville Island run by Chef Jamal, whose family previously ran the award-winning restaurants Rubina Tandoori and Tamarind Indian Bistro.

Although paneer originated in India, this curd cheese is the most consumed cheese in the traditional cuisine of all of South Asia, including Pakistan and Bangladesh. Buy fresh rennet-free paneer at Indian markets and use it within 3 to 4 days. If you cannot find paneer, substitute queso blanco, firm ricotta cheese or extra-firm tofu. Freezing or refrigerating this soup is not recommended. Ginger paste is peeled and sliced fresh ginger puréed with vegetable oil and can be refrigerated in an airtight container for up to 1 week.

ASIAN SALADS are very different from the vegetable or grain salads popular on Western menus. Whether hot or cold, most of the dishes called "salads" include pickles, vegetables, meat or cold cuts, seafood and seaweeds and even noodles. The biggest difference, however, is that Asians don't use salad dressings, since the salad ingredients already hold the flavour. You may find a few salads served with a dipping sauce to further enhance the taste.

Many of these salads, such as the Thai Green Papaya Salad and Japanese Marinated Spinach Salad, will be familiar; others, such as the Chinese Warm Jellyfish and Chicken Salad or the Twenty-First Century Salad, showcase newer, special recipes. Serve them family-style along with other more substantial dishes, or use them to start the meal. Koreans traditionally include at least four cold dishes (kimchi, daikon, dried fish, tofu or vegetables) at the beginning of the meal, northern Chinese often serve four, six or eight "small plates" of cold vegetables and/or meats to start, and Indians frequently offer finger foods and chutney once guests are seated.

SALADS

AND

APPETIZERS

GREEN PAPAYA SALAD
(Som Tom)
Serves 2 to 4

1 clove garlic, minced	4 cherry tomatoes, halved	1 cup fresh papaya, shredded
2 to 3 Thai chili peppers, chopped	1 Tbsp fish sauce	3 to 4 lettuce leaves
2 to 3 green beans, trimmed and julienned	1 Tbsp fresh lime juice	1 Tbsp crushed peanuts
	1 Tbsp white sugar	

ALTHOUGH ASIANS enjoy cooking with fruit, not too many varieties make it into recipes. Luckily, papaya is one of them. A great papaya salad must be impeccably fresh, not too sour and made with just the right amount of dressing so that it doesn't become soggy. SalaThai's version is made to order, and it's pure perfection.

Besides its use in salad, papaya is incorporated into soups, fried rice, stir fries and exquisite desserts. For this classic recipe, you need young papaya, which is available year-round in most markets. Choose plump, bright-green papayas with smooth, unblemished skins. The fruit's beige-yellow flesh should be firm and crisp, even when shredded.

IN A SMALL bowl, combine garlic, chili peppers, green beans and cherry tomatoes. Add fish sauce, lime juice and sugar, stirring well. Using a spatula, fold papaya into the vegetable mixture. If you prefer a cold salad, cover and refrigerate for 1 hour.

Line a small serving bowl with lettuce leaves. Spoon papaya salad on top and garnish with peanuts. Serve at room temperature.

Green (unripe) papaya

MARINATED SPINACH SALAD
(Gomae)

Serves 4

2 bunches spinach, rinsed
clean, stems attached

2 Tbsp dark shoyu

1 Tbsp rice vinegar

2 Tbsp shaved dry bonito flakes

1 Tbsp toasted white
sesame seeds

IN A LARGE flat pan, combine 4 cups water and 2 cups of ice. Set aside. Arrange paper towels on a clean work surface.

In a medium saucepan, bring 2 cups water to a boil on high heat. Blanch spinach for 30 seconds, then, using tongs, transfer immediately to the ice water bath. Allow spinach to soak for 1 minute until cold to the touch. Transfer spinach to the paper towels to drain, then place in a colander and, using your fingers, squeeze out any excess water.

Remove and discard spinach stems. Cut leaves into 2-inch lengths, place in a large bowl and gently separate individual leaves.

In a small bowl, combine shoyu, rice vinegar and bonito flakes and pour over spinach. Using a fork, gently mix the dressing into the spinach leaves and transfer to a serving bowl. Garnish with toasted sesame seeds. Serve cold.

WHEN IT comes to Japanese cuisine, both Chef Tojo and Tojo's are considered among the top names in Canada, if not in North America. Creator of the original California roll, Chef Tojo is known for his superb culinary skills and refined presentation and his insistence on using fresh, local products. A visit to his restaurant is guaranteed to be a memorable experience.

Shoyu is the top-grade Japanese soy sauce made with soy beans, cracked and roasted wheat, koji (mould grown on roasted cereal), salt and water, then fermented for 3 years and filtered. Dressing the cold spinach with shoyu and rice vinegar is a refreshing twist on the spinach gomae dressed with sesame paste and served by many Japanese eateries. Keep the spinach stems intact initially for easier handling after wilting. Enjoy this salad as a cold appetizer to a Japanese meal.

TWENTY-FIRST CENTURY SALAD

Serves 4 to 6

SESAME SALAD DRESSING	2 tsp white sugar	1 tsp cornstarch
6 Tbsp soy sauce, light or dark	1 Tbsp white sesame seeds	2 tsp sesame oil
6 Tbsp mirin	¼ cup balsamic vinegar	1 Tbsp extra-virgin olive oil
1 Tbsp sake		

BON APPÉTIT recently called Hapa one of the top five izakayas in North America. In Japanese, izakaya literally means "a place for food and drink," and these cozy casual dining rooms serving small plates of hot and cold dishes are very popular in Vancouver. But Hapa was the city's original izakaya, and it remains one of the best.

This vogue salad, a perennial bestseller, is a nourishing vegetarian meal that unites wholesome greens and hearty root vegetables with an aromatic sesame dressing. Welsh onions are Japanese green onions with thinner stalks but shorter, rounder bulbs.

Not counting the oil, soy sauce, sugar and water, the salad is made from a total of twenty-one ingredients—hence the name. Instead of deep-frying the potatoes and lotus root in this recipe, you can pan-fry them in ⅛ cup of oil for 4 to 5 minutes.

SESAME SALAD DRESSING In a small pot, combine soy sauce, mirin, sake, sugar, sesame seeds and balsamic vinegar and bring to a boil on medium-high.

In a small bowl, combine cornstarch and 2 Tbsp water until well mixed. Slowly pour into the soy sauce mixture, stirring gently for 15 to 20 seconds until thickened. Remove from the heat and allow to cool for 10 minutes.

Stir in sesame oil and olive oil and set aside.

CENTURY SALAD In a small pot, bring 2 cups water to a boil on high heat. Add carrots and blanch for 2 to 3 minutes, or until tender but crisp. Using a slotted spoon, transfer carrots to a medium bowl. Repeat with daikon, then with cauliflower, green beans and asparagus, blanching each vegetable separately for 2 to 3 minutes. Place vegetables together in one bowl and set aside.

In a wok or a deep fryer, heat canola oil to 300°F. Line a plate with paper towels. Add potatoes and cook for about 4 minutes until crisp and golden brown. Using a slotted spoon, transfer potatoes to the paper towel–lined plate to drain. Add lotus root to the wok (or deep fryer) and cook for about 4 minutes until crisp and golden. Transfer to the plate and allow to drain.

CENTURY SALAD

1 carrot, julienned	3 cups canola oil, for deep-frying	¼ yellow bell pepper, julienned
⅓ daikon, julienned	½ yellow-fleshed potato, shredded	1 stalk celery, julienned
⅓ cauliflower, chopped	⅓ lotus root, shredded	2 oz firm tofu, in ¾-inch dice
2 green beans, in 1-inch lengths	2 cups spring lettuce mix	3 cherry tomatoes, halved
2 asparagus, woody stems trimmed, in 1-inch lengths	¼ red bell pepper, julienned	½ cooked beet, finely shredded
	¼ green bell pepper, julienned	½ Welsh onion, finely shredded

In a large salad bowl, toss spring lettuce with 4 Tbsp sesame salad dressing. Arrange greens on a large serving platter.

To the blanched vegetables, add red, green and yellow bell peppers and celery. Add 2 Tbsp sesame salad dressing and toss well. Arrange vegetables in a ring around the outside of the platter. Top greens with tofu, tomatoes, beets and Welsh onions, then sprinkle with potato and lotus root chips. Pour the remaining sesame dressing into a small jug and serve with the salad. Serve immediately.

Refrigerate any leftover salad in an airtight container for up to 1 day.

Lotus root

YIN-YANG SALAD

Serves 4 to 6

3 slices ginger

one 8 oz skinless, boneless
chicken breast

1 tsp sesame oil

1 tsp light soy sauce

½ tsp oyster sauce

1 cup barbecued
duck meat, julienned

1 Tbsp finely chopped
pickled ginger

1 Tbsp hoisin sauce

1 Red Delicious apple, peeled,
cored and julienned

1 cup julienned
honeydew melon

1 cup julienned cantaloupe

1 Tbsp plain yogurt

1 tsp white sesame seeds

IN A SMALL saucepan, bring 2 cups water and ginger slices to a boil on high heat. Add chicken breast and cook for 2 minutes. Reduce the heat to low, cover and poach for 20 to 30 minutes. (To test for doneness, poke a knife into the thickest part of the breast. If the juices run clear, the meat is cooked through.) Discard the cooking water and ginger.

Transfer chicken to a strainer and place under cold running water for 2 to 3 minutes, or until chicken is cold to the touch. Turn off the water and allow chicken to drain for 10 minutes. Julienne the chicken meat.

In a medium bowl, toss chicken with sesame oil, soy sauce and oyster sauce and allow to marinate for about 15 minutes. Stir in duck meat, pickled ginger and hoisin sauce. Add apple, honeydew and cantaloupe, then gently fold in yogurt. Transfer salad to a serving platter, sprinkle with sesame seeds and serve immediately.

YIN-YANG IS an apt name for this dish that combines two distinctly flavoured and coloured poultry meats: the white poached chicken and the dark barbecued duck. This Westernized meat salad is based on a cold appetizer that originated in Hong Kong and was brought to Vancouver by Chinese chefs who immigrated in the late 1970s. It's a refreshing, summery salad served either as the first course of a meal or as an integral part of the appetizer platter for banquets.

Famous for its authentic dim sum, signature seafood dishes and roasted squab, Sun Sui Wah, which opened in the mid-1980s, was one of the first restaurants to build Vancouver's reputation for outstanding Asian food, and it continues to win awards and rave reviews across Canada and in Asia.

< *Twenty-First Century Salad (page 58)*

CURRIED CHICKEN SALAD
with Red and Green Bell Peppers (Chicken Choilaa)
Serves 4

8 oz skinless, boneless chicken thighs

1 tsp salt

1 medium onion, finely chopped

⅓ cup finely chopped green bell pepper

⅓ cup finely chopped red bell pepper

⅓ cup finely chopped carrots

1 tsp minced garlic

1 tsp minced ginger

1 Tbsp canola oil

½ tsp fenugreek seeds

½ Tbsp turmeric

½ Tbsp ground timur (or ground Szechuan peppercorns)

½ Tbsp ground cumin

½ Tbsp ground coriander

1 Tbsp fresh lemon juice

¼ cup coarsely chopped fresh cilantro

CAFÉ KATHMANDU is the first restaurant in Vancouver to serve authentic Nepalese dishes, such as this light and refreshing warm salad-style appetizer that is easy to make and shows just how simple Nepalese cooking can be.

Typical meals include rice, lentils and curries made with goat, pork, chicken and yak. Pickles and chutneys are popular accompaniments. If you can't find timur, a Himalayan peppercorn belonging to the Szechuan pepper family, use Szechuan peppercorns instead.

IN A SMALL POT, bring 2 cups water to a boil on high heat. Add chicken, reduce the heat to a simmer, cover and cook for 12 to 15 minutes, then drain and allow to cool for 10 to 15 minutes.

Using a knife, slice or shred the meat and place it in a large bowl. Season with salt, then add onions, green and red bell peppers, carrots, garlic and ginger. Mix well and set aside.

In a small frying pan, heat canola oil on medium-high and add fenugreek. Cook for 45 seconds, or until seeds become dark brown. Turn off the heat and stir in turmeric, mixing well. Pour the cooked spices over the chicken mixture, then stir in ground timur (or ground Szechuan peppercorns), cumin and coriander. Drizzle with lemon juice and garnish with cilantro. Serve on a large serving platter at room temperature.

WARM JELLYFISH AND CHICKEN SALAD

Serves 2 to 4

½ lb jellyfish, julienned

½ onion, sliced

one ½-inch-thick slice ginger

1 whole star anise

1 chicken leg, skin on

1 Tbsp dried shrimp

1 tsp minced garlic

1 Tbsp red rice vinegar

½ tsp Maggi sauce

¼ tsp sesame oil

1 sprig fresh cilantro, in 1-inch lengths

2 green onions, white part only, in 1-inch lengths

IN A SMALL POT, bring 1 cup water to a gentle boil. Add 1 cup cold water and jellyfish. Blanch for 20 seconds, then drain in a colander and rinse under cold running water for 2 minutes. Set aside and allow jellyfish to drain.

In a medium saucepan, bring 2 cups cold water, onions, ginger and star anise to a boil on high heat. Reduce the heat to medium-low and simmer for 10 minutes. Add chicken and poach for 20 to 30 minutes. (To test for doneness, poke a knife into the thickest part of the leg. If the juices run clear, the meat is cooked through.) Set the chicken and poaching liquid aside.

Combine 1 cup cold water and 1 cup ice cubes in a large bowl, then quickly plunge chicken leg into the ice water for 5 minutes. Drain off water and pat chicken dry with paper towels. Using a sharp knife, remove and discard skin and bones, then julienne the meat.

Set a fine-mesh sieve over a large, clean bowl. Pour the poaching liquid through the sieve, skimming off and discarding any fat. Ladle ½ cup of this clear broth back into the medium saucepan and set it on low heat. Add shrimp and simmer for 15 to 20 minutes until broth is reduced to about 1 Tbsp. Add garlic and vinegar and stir for 10 seconds. Remove from the heat and stir in jellyfish, chicken, Maggi sauce, sesame oil, cilantro and green onions. Serve at room temperature.

PREPARING JELLYFISH used to be a tedious, time-consuming task, making it a dine-out delicacy. These days, however, ready-to-cook packages of jellyfish are available at major Asian supermarkets, and so it's possible to enjoy them at home.

Jellyfish is most commonly served finely diced and tossed with soy sauce, sesame oil, salt and chili flakes. Brined and processed jellyfish is usually served as part of the appetizer platter at Chinese banquets. More recent recipes include pairings such as jellyfish and prawn salad, jellyfish and vegetable salad and this warm jellyfish and chicken salad, which showcases its gelatinous yet crunchy texture. Look for dried shrimp in plastic bags in the dried food aisle in Asian markets.

Made with water, salt, wheat gluten, sugar and other ingredients, Maggi sauce is a liquid seasoning produced by Nestlé. Many Asian chefs and homemakers refer to Maggi sauce as seasoned and sweetened soy sauce.

TRADITIONAL THAI MINCED CHICKEN SALAD
(Laab Gai)
Serves 2

2 Tbsp butter

1 Tbsp uncooked long-grain rice

10 oz finely minced raw white or dark chicken meat

1 Tbsp sliced red onion

2 Tbsp chopped fresh cilantro

½ Tbsp white sugar

1½ Tbsp fish sauce

¼ to ½ tsp roasted chili flakes

3 Tbsp fresh lime juice

1 Tbsp chopped green onions, white and green parts

6 fresh mint leaves

THIS TRADITIONAL Thai salad originated in the northeast of the country and is spicy, mildly sweet and full of finely chopped meat and fresh herbs. This version is from Thai House, one of the first Thai restaurants in Vancouver and the winner of many awards for its traditional and fusion dishes.

Pan-roasted rice grains provide crunchiness and substance in this salad, which can be enjoyed on its own as an appetizer or dressed up in a wrap as a quick meal.

IN A SMALL saucepan, heat 1 Tbsp of the butter on medium, then add rice and stir for 30 seconds Reduce the heat to low, cover and cook for 3 to 5 minutes, stirring every 30 seconds. The rice should turn brownish with a crispy coating. Transfer to a small bowl.

To the saucepan, add the remaining 1 Tbsp butter and chicken and sauté for 2 to 3 minutes. Turn off the heat.

In a medium bowl, combine rice, chicken, onions, cilantro, sugar, fish sauce and chili flakes, then add lime juice and mix well. Transfer to a serving bowl, garnish with green onions and mint leaves and serve warm.

Poached Chicken Salad with Butter-Braised Carrots and Chinese Celery (page 66) >

POACHED CHICKEN SALAD
with Butter-Braised Carrots and Chinese Celery
Serves 6 to 8

1 whole chicken, 2½ to 3 lbs	2 cloves garlic	2 cups Chinese celery, julienned
2 bunches green onions, whole + 2 green onions, white and green parts, minced	3 tsp salt	1 Tbsp peanut oil
	4 Tbsp butter	3 Tbsp black rice vinegar
½ lb ginger root, bruised + 3 Tbsp minced ginger	2 whole star anise	3 tsp light soy sauce
	5 white peppercorns	1 cup fresh cilantro leaves
1 bottle (600 mL/20 oz) Shaoxing rice wine	10 coriander seeds	
	1 large carrot, julienned	

ALTHOUGH A RELATIVE newcomer to Vancouver's Chinatown, Bao Bei has been getting rave reviews in local and national publications—including *Vancouver Magazine*, *The Georgia Straight*, *enRoute* magazine—and earning awards for its modern Asian dishes, fascinating drinks menu and chic interior design. It's known as the best modernized Asian food in B.C. that respects the culture and intent of the original dishes.

This hearty salad is derived from the traditional Chinese whole bone-in chicken, which is usually served as a delightful main dish—just bring out the rice! The earthy, leafy, herb-like Chinese celery used in this dish has thinner stems than regular celery and works charmingly with the buttery carrots.

PLACE CHICKEN IN a medium stockpot and add enough water to cover by an inch. Remove chicken and bring water to a boil on high heat. Blanch the chicken in boiling water for 5 seconds to tighten the skin and prevent splitting, then remove and set aside. To the pot of water, add whole green onions, bruised ginger root, wine, garlic and 1 tsp of the salt. When water boils again, reduce the heat to low, return chicken to the pot, cover and simmer for 30 minutes. Remove the pot from the heat and allow chicken to cool in the liquid to room temperature, about 90 minutes.

Transfer chicken to a large dish, cover tightly with plastic wrap and refrigerate for 1 hour. Strain poaching water through a strainer into a large, clean pot. Discard green onions, ginger and garlic. Cover chicken stock and refrigerate for 1 hour. Using a spoon, skim and discard fat from the stock. Measure 1 cup of stock and set aside (discard the rest).

In a small pot, heat butter, star anise, peppercorns and coriander seeds on medium heat until butter bubbles, about 1½ minutes. Using a spoon, remove and discard the spices. Add carrots, then ladle the 1 cup chicken stock overtop and add ½ tsp of the salt. Cover and cook on medium for 2 to 3 minutes until tender. Remove carrots from the heat and set aside.

Fill a large bowl with water and ice cubes. In another small pot, bring 1 cup water to a boil on high heat. Add ½ tsp of the salt and the Chinese celery and blanch for 90 seconds. Using tongs, plunge celery into the ice bath and allow to cool for 5 minutes. Drain celery in a colander and set aside.

In a small heatproof sauce bowl, combine minced green onion, minced ginger and the remaining 1 tsp salt. In a small saucepan, bring peanut oil to a boil on high heat. Slowly pour hot peanut oil into the ginger–green onion mixture, stir well and set aside.

In a small bowl, combine vinegar and soy sauce until well mixed.

To assemble the salad, arrange carrots and Chinese celery on a large serving platter. Remove chicken from the refrigerator, then unwrap, chop into bite-size pieces through the bone and arrange on top of the vegetables. Drizzle the vinegar–soy sauce mixture over the chicken and garnish with cilantro leaves. Serve the ginger–green onion sauce over the chicken or as a dipping sauce on the side.

Refrigerate leftover chicken salad in an airtight container for up to 2 days.

CHINATOWN

VANCOUVER'S ORIGINAL CHINATOWN is located in the area bounded by Main and Pender, Keefer and Georgia Streets, and although it's not half as busy as it once was (now that many Chinese have moved out to Richmond and Burnaby), it's still a great place to take in the sights, sounds and smells of Asia. Hanging in the window of meat shops such as Dollar Meats, Chinatown's oldest meat and barbecue shop, are two-hundred-pound roasted pigs alongside barbecued ducks. Strands of prosciutto-like Chinese-style ham dangle from the rafters, and display cases of Chinese bacon, sausages and sun-dried meats fill the store.

Around the corner are popular Asian groceries, such as Chinatown Supermarket, where boxes of loose Asian greens and pyramids of fragrant mangoes and longans and durian are neatly and colourfully arranged by the entrance. Do as the locals do, and get close, look, feel and touch the produce to inspect its freshness. Inside are shelves of condiments and other Asian foods. Also around the corner are herbal stores such as Guo Hua, where you can browse the jars and bins of dried teas, herbs and medicines, as well as seeds and flowers, nuts and dried fruits, dried seafood and dried insects, too.

In Chinatown, follow the smell of freshly steamed Chinese buns to Sun Fresh Bakery, where the fluffy white breads are baked throughout the day. Take a tea break in Maxim's Bakery or The Boss Bakery and Restaurant, one of the signature Hong Kong–style cafés and bakeries: help yourself to a cup of hot or cold yin-yang (tea and coffee served in one cup) and bite into one of the Chinese cakes stuffed with sweet paste or a European-style baked pastry such as a cocktail bun, an egg tart or a char siu roll. Admire the Chinese wedding (dragon and phoenix) cakes and the beautifully dressed fresh mango and cream cakes.

Other hidden gems in Chinatown include Phnom Penh, one of the city's best Vietnamese and Cambodian restaurants, known for chicken wings and butter beef and steaming bowls of pho'. Nearby is Hon's, the original won ton house in Chinatown, which now produces a huge array of noodles for its restaurants and for retail sale. And not far away is Jade Dynasty, which serves authentic dim sum and is especially crowded at lunchtime. You may well see one of the generation of Chinese elders who still bank, shop and socialize in the area, picking up Chinese pastries, groceries or hot food to take home. Who can give up the convenience and great pricing of shopping in Chinatown?

Chinatown may be at its best during the day, but on weekend summer evenings, time your visit to take in the Vancouver Chinatown Night Market that sets up right on the street. Among the stalls selling clothing and electronics and handicrafts are hawkers making and selling delicious street food such as fish balls on skewers, dim sum and pastries. There's also great new night-time energy in the area thanks to the opening of Bao Bei Chinese Brasserie and the Keefer Bar, hip, modern eateries that honour Chinatown's past but bring it firmly into the present.

CHAWAN MUSHI WITH SHRIMP AND DUNGENESS CRAB
(Egg Custard with Shrimp and Dungeness Crab)
Serves 4

3 oz chicken thigh meat, in ½-inch dice

1 Tbsp + ½ tsp light soy sauce

½ tsp sake

½ tsp sea salt

4 shrimp, peeled, deveined and halved

2 oz fresh enoki mushrooms

4 oz cooked Dungeness crabmeat, picked over for cartilage

4 to 8 ginkgo nuts, peeled

4 medium eggs

2½ cups dashi (page 110) (or light chicken stock)

1 Tbsp mirin

1 tsp yuzu juice (optional)

1 tsp natural tobiko

BOTH JAPANESE and Chinese have always enjoyed steamed savoury custards as part of their homemade meals. In China they are called *jing dan* and, in Japan, *chawan mushi*. The silky-smooth chawan mushi served at Tojo's is loaded with elegant ingredients, including indigenous B.C. Dungeness crabmeat, shrimp and tobiko (flying fish roe).

This dish is traditionally made by steaming the ingredients in chawan mushi cups. If you do not have any, use small ramekins or heatproof teacups instead. Instead of steaming, you can place the cups in a bain-marie and cook them in a preheated 425°F oven for 30 minutes or until the custard is set.

IN A SMALL bowl, combine chicken, ½ tsp soy sauce and sake and allow to marinate for about 15 minutes. Drain off the excess liquid and set aside.

In a small saucepan, bring 1 cup water and sea salt to a boil on high heat. Add shrimp and blanch for 30 seconds. Using a slotted spoon, transfer shrimp to a colander and allow to drain. Set aside.

Trim and discard 1½ inches from bottom of mushrooms and separate by hand. Cut into 1-inch lengths.

In a wok fitted with a bamboo steamer or in a covered steamer, bring 4 to 5 cups water to a gentle boil on high heat. Among 4 chawan mushi cups, evenly divide chicken, shrimp, mushrooms, crabmeat and ginkgo nuts.

In a large bowl, beat eggs. Slowly stir in dashi (or chicken stock), 1 Tbsp soy sauce, ½ tsp salt and mirin. Using a small fine-mesh strainer, skim any foam or air bubbles from the surface and discard. Ladle the dashi mixture into the chawan mushi cups, leaving about ½ inch clear at the top. Place lids on chawan mushi cups (or, if using ramekins or teacups, tightly seal with industrial-strength plastic wrap or aluminum foil).

Arrange chawan mushi cups in the bamboo steamer
or on the steamer rack. Tightly seal the steamer with
a piece of aluminum foil or with the lid and steam for
about 20 minutes on medium heat. (To test for doneness,
insert a toothpick in the middle of the custard; if it comes
out clean, the custard is ready.) Garnish each serving
with a few drops of yuzu juice and ¼ tsp tobiko. Serve
immediately.

STUFFED TOMATOES WITH GROUND PRAWNS

Serves 6 to 8

1 lb prawns, cleaned, deveined and cut in ½-inch dice

½ tsp salt

1 tsp white sugar

½ tsp freshly ground white pepper

1 egg white, beaten

1 Tbsp tapioca flour

6 to 8 Roma tomatoes, halved horizontally

3 Tbsp cornstarch

1 Tbsp vegetable oil

1 tsp tomato paste

¼ cup chicken stock

1 tsp red rice vinegar

1 Tbsp raw crabmeat, picked over for cartilage

1 Tbsp chopped green onions, white and green parts

SUN SUI WAH is a second-generation restaurant, based on a renowned Chinese eating establishment of the same name in Hong Kong. Vancouverites and visitors to the city flock to this fine-dining restaurant for dim sum and seafood dishes, including Alaska King Crab sumptuously prepared in multiple courses. Now considered one of the top ten places for Asian food in Vancouver, the extensive menu features lavish dishes made from live seafood and local, seasonal products.

Prawns, when seasoned and ground to a paste, are called *ha gaw* by Chinese chefs, not to be confused with the shrimp dumplings called *ha gou*. This is the esteemed filling for quite a few Cantonese delicacies, such as stuffed crab claws, stuffed mushrooms and stuffed oysters.

IN A MEDIUM bowl, combine prawns with salt, ½ tsp of the sugar, white pepper, egg white and tapioca flour until well coated. Transfer the prawn mixture to a large, thick cutting board and, using the back of a cleaver or a meat pounder, grind for about 10 minutes or until the mixture becomes a paste. (Manually grinding the prawns rather than blitzing them in the food processor gradually releases the fat, which makes the paste fluffier and more elastic and allows it to bind better.) Transfer the prawn paste to a bowl and set aside.

Using a teaspoon, gently scoop out tomato seeds and pulp, leaving ¼ inch of pulp around the sides and ½ inch at the base. Discard the seeds and tomato pulp (or reserve them for another use). Evenly fill each tomato half with shrimp paste, gently pressing it down with the teaspoon.

Place the cornstarch on a small, shallow plate. In a large nonstick frying pan, heat vegetable oil on medium-high. Lightly dip the prawn side of the stuffed tomatoes into the cornstarch to coat the surface. Shake off any excess and place prawn side down in the pan. When all tomatoes are in the pan, pan-fry for another 30 seconds, then reduce the heat to medium-low and allow them to cook while you prepare the sauce.

In a medium bowl, combine tomato paste, chicken stock, vinegar and the remaining ½ tsp sugar. Using a whisk, whip for 45 seconds, then slowly add to the pan, cover and cook for 1 minute. Add crabmeat, bring to a gentle boil and reduce the heat to medium.

In a small bowl, mix the remaining cornstarch with 2 Tbsp cold water. Slowly stir the cornstarch mixture into the pan and cook for 20 to 30 seconds, until the sauce thickens. Transfer tomatoes and crabmeat sauce to a deep serving dish, sprinkle with green onions and serve hot.

KOREAN-STYLE BBQ PORK LETTUCE WRAPS

Makes about 25 wraps

3½ oz coarse salt

1 cup white sugar

1 bone-in pork shoulder, 4 to 5 lbs

1 cup brown sugar

2 green onions, white and green parts, in ⅛-inch dice

4 oz ginger, peeled, in ⅛-inch dice

2 cups napa cabbage kimchi

5 oz roasted peanuts, crushed

⅜ cup soy sauce

¼ to ½ cup vinegar-based chili sauce (optional)

2 heads lettuce, rinsed, drained, separated and cut in palm-size pieces

½ cup cooked long-grain white rice

EVEN VANCOUVER'S chain restaurants, such as Cactus Club, are embracing Asian flavours! This is a gluten-free meal from Canadian Iron Chef Rob Feenie that features Korean ingredients. Other Asian gems on the Cactus Club menu include wor wonton, tuna tataki, Szechuan green beans, edamame and teriyaki rice bowl.

This "make-your own" appetizer is a feast that can go around the table all night long. The pork shoulder requires overnight curing and hours of slow baking. It's the only item that takes time but is quite easy to attend to. The actual preparation time is minimal, and the end result is so worth it. For this recipe, use kimchi made with napa cabbage. And for the lettuce wraps, try iceberg, romaine or Chinese leaf lettuce (a thin, leafy lettuce available in Chinese grocery stores). Refrigerate the lettuce until meal time.

IN A BOWL, combine salt and white sugar. Using your fingers, rub this cure mixture evenly onto pork. Place pork in a large bowl or container, cover and refrigerate for a minimum of 6 hours.

Uncover pork and discard any liquid. Rinse pork under cold running water to remove excess cure mixture.

Preheat the oven to 275°F and place pork, fat cap up, in a roasting pan. Add 2 cups water and cover with aluminum foil. Roast for 7 hours.

Remove and discard the foil and sprinkle pork with brown sugar. Return pork to the oven and roast for 1 more hour, basting every 15 minutes.

Remove pork from the oven and allow to rest for 15 minutes. Pour off any liquid. Transfer pork to a large plate and, using two spoons, shred the meat. Place pulled pork in a bowl and set aside.

In a small sauce bowl, combine green onions and ginger. Place kimchi in a medium serving bowl and, using scissors, cut it into small pieces. Pour peanuts, soy sauce and chili sauce into 3 separate serving bowls. Arrange pulled pork and lettuce leaves in 2 separate piles on a large serving platter. Mound rice in a serving bowl. Set the bowls of rice and condiments around the platter. Pass around individual plates and encourage guests to serve

themselves by placing a leaf of lettuce flat on the plate, mounding 2 to 3 Tbsp pulled pork on top and dressing it with condiments as desired. Fold the bottom of the leaf over the filling, then tuck in the sides like an envelope. Fold the top of the leaf over the filling and enjoy.

Refrigerate any leftover pork, rice, condiments and lettuce leaves separately in airtight containers for up to 2 days.

I N CHINA, dainty handmade dumplings, savoury morsels and delicate pastries are referred to as dim sum, which translates as "touch the heart" but actually means "snacks." Originally prepared for royal families, nobility and other well-to-dos, dim sum is a form of culinary art. Chinese call the dim sum gathering *"yum cha,"* a time to socialize, enjoy a light meal and drink tea—traditional tea houses often offer individually selected blends, freshly brewed and served in ceramic cups—with the food being secondary. This "meal" is usually served as early as dawn or in the middle of the day, and diners order by ticking off boxes on a special menu or pointing to the dishes they want as the food is wheeled around on carts. Dim sum now often refers to small bites of food, eaten quickly as a snack.

Although dim sum is specifically Chinese, snacks are available across Asia in street stalls and night markets and bus and train stations, to eat on the spot or take away. Steaming hot, served on skewers or folded into paper, these are the roasted meats, grilled vegetables and fried cakes whose sweet, spicy and salty aromas draw you in. Try the irresistible deep-fried Cantonese Won Tons and Tofu and Crabmeat Pockets or the baked Shami (Spicy Chicken) Kebabs or Smoky Tea Sauce with Hard-Boiled Eggs and Toast.

DIM SUM **AND** SNACKS

TOFU AND CRABMEAT POCKETS

Makes about 40 pockets

4 cups + 1 Tbsp vegetable oil

1 tsp finely chopped ginger
+ 1 tsp minced ginger

1 block plain medium tofu,
in ¾-inch dice

5 oz canned straw mushrooms,
drained and chopped

2 oz cooked crabmeat,
picked over for cartilage

1 Tbsp finely chopped green onions,
white and green parts

Ground white pepper to taste

40 fresh won ton wrappers,
each 3 ½ inches square

1 Tbsp red rice vinegar

1 Tbsp light soy sauce

NORTHERN DELICACY is a bright, roomy Mandarin Chinese restaurant in Richmond's Aberdeen Mall, where diners can watch Chef Yip handcraft dainty *xiao long bao* (juicy pork dumplings), potstickers and other dim sum dishes. These crunchy golden pockets are hard to resist once the nutty flavour of the soft tofu and sweetness of the succulent crabmeat explode in your mouth. They're a great finger food and pair well with cold sake, beer and chilled white wine.

Tofu is a common ingredient in many Asian recipes because of its versatility, especially in vegan dishes. Whether it's pressed, firm, medium or soft, tofu can be found in soups, appetizers, snacks, entrées and even desserts. Buying double packs of tofu costs a lot less than purchasing single blocks. To store unused tofu, remove it from the original package and place it in an airtight container. Fill the container with fresh cold tap water, renewing it every 3 days, and refrigerate for up to 10 days. These pockets don't store well once cooked, so try to avoid leftovers.

IN A WOK, heat 1 Tbsp vegetable oil on high heat. Add chopped ginger, tofu and mushrooms, stir gently and cook for 1 minute. Add crabmeat and green onions, season with salt and freshly ground white pepper and cook for 30 seconds. Transfer this tofu mixture to a bowl and allow to cool for 15 minutes. Pour off any liquid in the bowl.

Place 4 Tbsp cold water in a small bowl. Lightly dust a baking sheet with cornstarch. Arrange a won ton wrapper on a clean, dry work surface with one of the corners toward you. (Keep the remaining wrappers covered with a damp towel.) Using a spoon, mound 1 Tbsp of the tofu mixture in the centre of the wrapper. Dip your index finger in the bowl of cold water, then run it around the edge of the wrapper to moisten. Fold the bottom half of the dough over the filling to make a triangle. Press the edges together gently to seal them. Transfer the filled pocket to the baking sheet. Repeat with the remaining wrappers and tofu mixture.

Line a wire rack with paper towels. In a wok or a deep fryer, heat 4 cups vegetable oil to 350°F. To test that the oil is hot enough, carefully add one pocket. If the pocket rises to the top almost immediately, the oil is ready. Cook the pockets in batches to prevent overcrowding. Gently place 8 to 10 pockets in the oil and cook for 3 to 4 minutes, or until they rise to the surface. Use a slotted spoon to transfer the cooked pockets to the paper towel–lined wire rack to drain.

In a small bowl, combine vinegar, soy sauce and minced ginger until well mixed. Transfer to a sauce bowl. Arrange the tofu pockets on a serving platter and serve with this dipping sauce.

SMOKY TEA SAUCE
with Hard-Boiled Eggs and Toast

Serves 3 to 4

2 cinnamon sticks	4 tsp Chinese black tea leaves	15 to 20 slices baguette, toasted and lightly buttered
3 whole star anise	2 cups filtered water	
5 whole cloves	1 cup packed dark brown sugar	2 to 3 hard-boiled eggs, in ⅛-inch slices
	⅛ tsp soy sauce	

IN NORTHERN China, eggs, still in their shells, are boiled in a tea-infused liquid for hours and enjoyed as part of a traditional breakfast or a savoury snack. This recipe is a variation on that idea: instead of boiling the eggs in tea, Chef Ma produces a thick, syrupy tea-flavoured sauce made with her own Main Street Breakfast black tea, which is served with hard-boiled eggs and buttered toast. Leftover sauce can be refrigerated in an airtight container for up to 10 days.

MAKE A SPICE sachet by placing a 4-inch square piece of cheesecloth on a clean work surface. Arrange cinnamon sticks, star anise and cloves in the middle of the cheesecloth. Gather the corners of the cheesecloth, completely encasing the spices, and tie tightly with a piece of kitchen twine. Repeat with a second piece of cheesecloth and the black tea leaves to make another sachet.

In a medium saucepan, combine the filtered water, brown sugar and both sachets and bring to a boil on high heat. Reduce to a simmer, cover and cook for 30 minutes.

Using a spoon, remove the tea sachet and allow it to cool slightly. Place the sachet in a small bowl and, using two spoons, squeeze out as much liquid as possible. Pour the liquid back into the saucepan and discard the tea leaves.

Simmer the tea mixture for another 20 minutes, then remove and discard the spice sachet. Increase the heat to medium-low and simmer the mixture for 30 to 40 minutes until reduced to a thick syrup. Remove from the heat and gently stir in soy sauce, then allow to cool to room temperature.

Spread tea sauce on toast and serve with sliced hard-boiled eggs.

THE BLOCKS ON Main Street between 48th and 51st Avenues are known for their colourful fabric stores and bazaars as well as an abundance of Indian spice shops, grocery stores and authentic sweet shops and restaurants. This is Vancouver's Little India.

Halal Meats and Poultry is a great place to buy very inexpensive meats, including hard-to-find cuts of goat and other less common animals. Peruse the Punjabi Food Market, which is well stocked with beans, lentils and spices, and bags of onions and garlic that lie at the front of the store. Fruiticana is a large supermarket chain that sells kitchen tools and cookware. With the smell of curry wafting down the street, and the aroma of oven-fresh samosas, it won't take long to find somewhere to eat. All India Sweets is famous for its desserts: rows and rows of sticky, multicoloured barfi (fudge) and gulab jamen (dumplings in syrup). It also features an all-you-can-eat vegetarian buffet. Frequented by locals who live in the neighbourhood, this area remains busy with businesspeople and homemakers with their kids during the week and will always be the ultimate dining and shopping haven for families on the weekends.

Also popular and in the area are the two similarly named tandoori restaurants. Tandoori King is located on Fraser Street near Marine Drive, whereas Original Tandoori K. King is an unassuming place around the corner on East 65th. They are two of the oldest tandoori restaurants in the city, and one taste of the assorted tandoori platter or the oven-fresh naan will leave no doubt as to why.

Not in the area, but consistently ranked as the best contemporary Indian food in the city is Vij's and its sister restaurant, Rangoli, located on 11th Avenue at Granville. Try the decadent Lamb Popsicles or the rich and delicious Portobello Mushrooms and Red Bell Peppers in Creamy Curry.

BEAN CURD, MUSHROOM, CARROT AND CELERY WRAPS

Makes two 8- to 10-inch-long wraps

1 small carrot, in ⅛-inch slices	4 shiitake mushrooms, julienned	½ tsp freshly ground white pepper
2 Tbsp light soy sauce	2 stalks celery, julienned	1 tsp sesame oil
3 slices ginger, peeled and chopped	2 tsp oyster sauce	2 semi-dry bean curd sheets, each 16 inches
3 Tbsp vegetable oil	½ tsp salt	1 to 2 Tbsp red rice vinegar or Worcestershire sauce
	1 tsp white sugar	

THIS CRISPY pan-fried vegetarian roll locals call *su-uh* is served as a dim sum item in Mandarin restaurants. It can also be enjoyed as an appetizer. Although the dim sum menu at New Westminster's Spring Garden is small compared with other Chinese restaurants, it features these delicious wraps, as well as top-notch chicken feet and pan-fried daikon cakes.

Instead of won ton or spring roll wrappers, this dish uses 16-inch-wide, semi-dry oval bean curd sheets, which are available in packages at Chinese grocery stores and most Asian markets. Thin and ready to use, each sheet is perfect for making one wrap. Do not remove the sheets from the package until you are ready to use them, as they dry out quickly. To save time, you can make these wraps ahead of time and freeze them, uncooked, in an airtight container for up to a week.

IN A SMALL microwave-safe bowl, toss carrots with 1 Tbsp of the soy sauce and ginger. Microwave for 2 minutes on medium-high. Allow to cool for 5 minutes, then discard ginger and julienne carrots.

In a wok, heat 1 Tbsp of the vegetable oil on high, then add mushrooms, celery, the remaining 1 Tbsp soy sauce, oyster sauce, salt and sugar and sauté for 1 minute. Stir in carrots, white pepper and sesame oil. Transfer the vegetable mixture to a bowl and allow it to rest for 15 minutes.

Place a bean curd sheet on a clean, dry work surface or a large cutting board. If the sheet is folded, open it gently. Using a clean wet towel, lightly moisten both sides. Place half the vegetable mixture in a line along the bottom of the bean curd sheet, about 2 inches from the edge and the two sides. Using a spoon, flatten and spread the mixture evenly across the bottom half of the sheet. Fold the bottom edge of the sheet over the filling, enclosing the vegetable mixture, then tightly roll the sheet away from you once more. Tuck in the sides like an envelope, then continue rolling until you reach the end of the bean curd sheet. Repeat with the second sheet and the remaining vegetable mixture.

Fresh shiitake mushrooms

In a 14-inch frying pan, heat the remaining 2 Tbsp vegetable oil on medium-high. Gently place the bean curd wraps in the pan, seam side down, and reduce the heat to medium. Pan-fry for 3 to 4 minutes, or until the wraps are light brown. Using a spatula, press and flatten the wraps gently. Flip the wraps over and pan-fry them for another 2 to 3 minutes.

Transfer the wraps to a clean, dry cutting board, allow them to rest for 3 to 4 minutes, then cut them into 1½-inch lengths. Arrange the wraps on a long platter. Pour vinegar or Worcestershire sauce into a dipping bowl and serve with the wraps.

STEAMED PORK AND CABBAGE BUNS

Makes 20 to 24 buns

STEAMED BUN DOUGH	
9 cups sifted all-purpose flour	1¼ cups white sugar
2 tsp baking powder	⅜ cup shortening, cubed (about 3 oz)
4 Tbsp fresh yeast	2 cups hot water (135°F)
½ tsp salt	

IN THE northern and western regions of China, steamed buns—known in Mandarin as *jing bao*—are the main source of protein and carbohydrates. Elsewhere they are an indulgence for many Chinese food lovers. Steamed buns have a beautiful round shape, a smooth surface and a sweet yeast flavour. Their fillings can be savoury or sweet. Sun Fresh Bakery makes its buns throughout the day, and they are soft and fluffy with generous portions of irresistible fillings. Those in the know flock to this Keefer Street institution and buy them by the dozen. Whole wheat varieties are also available.

If you have more than one steamer, stack them one on top of the other and steam the buns all at the same time by covering the top steamer. If you only have one steamer, simply steam the buns in batches. Steamed buns can be frozen in resealable plastic bags for up to 2 weeks. (When reheating them in the microwave, fill a small microwave-safe bowl with water and place it beside the buns; cook on medium-high heat for 1 minute.)

STEAMED BUN DOUGH In a large bowl, combine flour, baking powder, yeast, salt and sugar. Using two knives, cut in shortening until ingredients are well mixed and smooth.

Slowly stir in ¼ cup hot water to moisten the dry ingredients. Gradually add more water while gently kneading the dough, until it just holds together. Continue kneading for 15 to 20 minutes until the dough feels dry to the hand. Allow the dough to rest for 20 minutes.

PORK AND CABBAGE FILLING Place cabbage in a microwave-safe bowl, cover and cook on high for 2 to 3 minutes. Allow to cool for 10 minutes, then drain in a colander and roll in dry towels to remove any excess moisture.

In a large bowl, combine cabbage, pork, salt, sugar, soy sauce, sesame oil and cornstarch until well mixed. Set aside.

FINISH STEAMED BUNS Lightly dust a clean work surface with flour. Cut twenty-four 3-inch squares of parchment paper.

Divide the dough into 24 equal pieces. Roll each piece between your hands to create a ball. Using a rolling pin, roll each ball into a circle ¼ inch thick and 5 inches in diameter.

PORK AND CABBAGE FILLING

1½ lbs Taiwanese cabbage (gao-li choy), chopped

1½ lbs raw ground pork

1½ Tbsp salt

1½ Tbsp white sugar

2 Tbsp soy sauce

3 Tbsp sesame oil

2 Tbsp cornstarch

Holding the dough in one hand, spoon 2 Tbsp stuffing into the centre, then cup your palm so that the dough forms a bowl shape around the filling. With your other hand, gather the edges of the dough toward the centre to completely encase the filling. Press the edges of the dough together with your fingers and twist them into a small knob. Gently place the bun, knob side up, on a square of parchment paper and set it on a baking sheet. Fill and shape the remaining buns, then cover with a clean, dry cloth and allow to rise for 45 to 60 minutes until almost doubled in size.

Arrange buns in large bamboo steamers, leaving 1 inch around each one so that they don't stick together. In a large wok, bring 2 cups water to a boil on high heat, set steamer on top (make sure the water is boiling), cover and steam for 20 minutes. Remove from the heat and allow to cool for 3 to 5 minutes with the lid on to prevent the buns from collapsing. Serve immediately.

CANTONESE WON TONS

Serves 6 to 8 (Makes 70 to 80 won tons)

10 oz pork butt meat, minced or ground

1 lb prawns, cleaned, deveined and cut in ½-inch dice

2 egg whites

1½ tsp salt

½ tsp ground white pepper

2 Tbsp vegetable oil

1 Tbsp all-purpose flour

70 to 80 won ton wrappers, each 3½ inches square

¼ cup chopped green onions, white and green parts

¼ cup chopped fresh cilantro

1 Tbsp light soy sauce

1 tsp sesame oil

1 Tbsp chili oil (optional)

WON TONS, the filled dumplings that are the best-known and most widespread Chinese food, have been around since the Han Dynasty (206 BC–AD 220). Many people mistakenly believe the word pronounced "won ton" in Cantonese literally means "swallowing clouds," whereas others say the name refers to its cloud shape when cooked. However, won tons were originally a Mandarin dim sum, and their name, when written, had nothing to do with either "swallowing" or "clouds." The first Chinese character, "won," combines the notion of eating and the rolling pin, while the second character, "ton," pairs the idea of eating with immediacy. Thus, the original meaning of this Chinese word conveys both the act of making won tons and eating them as soon as they're cooked!

Chinese Bistro is the newest Chinese restaurant in Whistler—and the one and only that serves both modern and authentic Chinese cuisine. Northern Chinese won tons contain pork and/or vegetables; the smaller Cantonese food cart–style (*dai-pai-dong*) won tons, like these ones, are stuffed with mostly minced pork and diced prawns. You can freeze uncooked won tons in an airtight container for up to one week.

IN A MEDIUM bowl, combine pork and prawns. Fold in egg whites, ½ tsp of the salt, white pepper, 1½ Tbsp of the vegetable oil and flour and mix well.

Lightly dust a baking sheet with cornstarch. Arrange a won ton wrapper on a clean, dry work surface (keep the remaining wrappers covered with a damp towel). Using a butter knife, spoon 2 tsp of the filling onto the middle of the wrapper. Gently gather together the 4 corners of the wrapper, encasing the filling, then twist the corners together lightly to form a sealed pouch. Place the won ton on the baking sheet. Repeat with the remaining wrappers and filling.

Divide green onions and cilantro among 6 to 8 individual serving bowls.

In a medium stockpot, bring 8 cups water to a boil on high heat. Add ½ Tbsp vegetable oil and remaining 1 tsp salt. Using a slotted spoon, place 20 to 25 won tons into the water, being careful not to overcrowd the pot. (Overcrowding prevents the won tons from boiling properly and may cause them to stick together.) Boil for 6 to 7 minutes, or until won tons float to the top.

Using a slotted spoon, remove cooked won tons and divide them evenly among the serving bowls. Repeat as necessary, until all won tons are cooked.

In a small sauce bowl, combine soy sauce, sesame oil and chili oil until well mixed. Serve on the side as a dipping sauce.

MUNG BEAN PANCAKES

Makes 8 to 10 pancakes

1 pkg (400 g) skinned split dry mung beans

1 medium onion, thinly sliced

½ carrot, julienned

3 green onions, white and green parts, julienned + 2 tsp chopped green onions

2 oz ground pork (optional)

½ cup kimchi, julienned

¼ cup bean sprouts, blanched and roughly chopped

2 Tbsp salt

6 Tbsp vegetable oil

3 Tbsp light soy sauce

IN A MEDIUM saucepan, cover mung beans with 3 to 4 cups cold water, or enough to cover the beans by ½ inch, and allow to soak for 1 hour.

Transfer beans and their soaking water to a food processor. Blend on low for 3 minutes, then increase the speed to high and blend for 5 to 6 minutes, or until the mixture becomes a smooth paste.

In a medium bowl, combine onions, carrots, julienned green onions, pork, kimchi and bean sprouts. Using a spatula, fold in mung bean paste. Add salt and 2 Tbsp water and mix well.

In a nonstick pan, heat 1 Tbsp of the vegetable oil on medium-high. Using a ladle, drop about ⅓ cup batter into the pan and swirl it to create an even 5- to 6-inch pancake about ¼ inch thick. Cook for about 90 seconds, then turn pancake over and cook for another 90 seconds, or until golden brown. Transfer to a platter, cover with a tea towel to keep warm and set aside. Add a few drops of oil to the pan, then repeat with the remaining batter. You should have about 8 to 10 pancakes.

In a small bowl, combine soy sauce and chopped green onions.

Serve pancakes on a platter and pass the dipping sauce.

LANGLEY MAY seem like a long way to go for Korean food, but the opening of an H-Mart Asian grocery store in this city shows how the Korean population is growing in Surrey and Langley. Buk Jang Do Ga, which means "an assembly of Korean drums," is known for its homestyle cooking, especially such dishes as its catfish sautéed in kimchi and bean sprouts.

Savoury pancakes, loaded with hearty ingredients, are a classic Korean home-cooked meal. Churning mung beans into a smooth paste at home is easier than you think. Buy skinned, split mung beans in 400-gram packages, which are readily available in most Asian grocery stores.

DAIKON, SCALLION AND POTATO PANCAKES

Serves 4 to 6

2 cups daikon, shredded	2 tsp salt
2 cups yellow potato, shredded and towel dried	1 large egg
6 green onions, white and green parts, shredded	4 to 6 Tbsp canola oil

ALANA PECKHAM is a Vancouver-born and -raised Chinese with French culinary training and extensive experience working in local fine-dining restaurants. She brings French, Chinese and Pacific Northwest sensibilities to all of her dishes.

Daikon cake, steamed or pan-fried, is a popular dim sum item in Cantonese restaurants because of its pudding-like texture and mildly sweet flavour, just as a pan-fried scallion (green onion) pancake is hard to pass up in Mandarin restaurants because of its crisp texture and aromatic flavour. Combining the two and adding yellow potato gives these wholesome, easy-to-make vegetarian pancakes a golden colour and crisp texture like hash browns. Make them fresh and serve them with tea or soy milk as an appetizer, a side dish or a snack.

IN A MEDIUM saucepan, bring 3 cups water to a rolling boil on high heat. Add daikon and blanch for 2 minutes, then drain and allow to cool for 5 minutes. Using your hands, squeeze as much liquid from the daikon as you can. Place daikon on a clean tea towel and roll tightly to extract any remaining moisture so that the batter does not become runny. Unroll the tea towel and pat dry.

In a medium bowl, stir together daikon, potatoes, green onions, salt and egg, folding the mixture until well combined.

Heat a frying pan on medium and add 1 Tbsp canola oil. Ladle 4 Tbsp of the batter onto the pan and cook for 2 minutes, or until golden brown. Using a turner, flip cake over and cook for another 2 minutes, or until golden brown and crispy. Repeat, adding more canola oil to the pan as necessary, with the remaining batter. You should have 15 to 20 pancakes. Serve immediately.

Wrap leftover pancakes in aluminum foil and refrigerate for up to 3 days.

TOKYO-STYLE CRÊPES

Makes 4 crêpes

¾ cup all-purpose flour

3 Tbsp tapioca flour

2 Tbsp wheat starch

2 large eggs

1 cup homogenized milk

2 Tbsp butter, in ½-inch cubes

½ tsp vanilla extract

3 Tbsp white sugar

3 oz hand-peeled cooked shrimp

1 tsp fresh lemon juice

2 oz cooked ham, julienned

3 oz hard cheese of your choice, shredded

4 tsp Japanese (kewpie) mayonnaise

3 fresh basil (or mint) leaves, chopped

WHEN CHRISTIANITY and Western culture were introduced to Japan during the feudal era in the mid 1700s, that country also acquired European foods and cooking techniques. In turn, 50 years of Japanese rule over Taiwan, from the late nineteenth to the mid-twentieth century, left its own culinary mark: Japanese dishes and some European-influenced recipes, too. Modern Taiwanese cafés serve cross-cultural cuisine and bento-style meals, including this delicious but unusual crêpe.

Dessert Dynasty was the first bubble tea café to open in Metro Vancouver, in 1994. It still serves up trendy bubble teas, its famous made-to-order egg-bubble waffles and addictive crêpes. Turn this recipe into a dessert crêpe by replacing the shrimp, ham and cheese with an equal amount of fruit, such as cubed berries, mango, melons and bananas. Replace the mayonnaise with whipped cream and the basil (or mint) with ½ tsp brown sugar.

IN A BLENDER, combine all-purpose, tapioca and wheat flours, eggs, milk, butter, vanilla and sugar and blend for 3 to 5 minutes until well mixed. Set aside at room temperature for at least 1 hour to allow the batter to settle to the correct consistency.

In a small bowl, toss shrimp with lemon juice and divide among 4 small bowls. Evenly divide ham and cheese among the 4 bowls.

Heat a 10-inch nonstick pan on high. To test that the pan is hot enough, drizzle a few drops of water in the centre. If the water sizzles, ladle 4 Tbsp batter into the pan, swirling it around to make an even, thin crêpe 8 inches in diameter. Reduce the heat to medium and cook for 2 minutes. Arrange the shrimp, ham and cheese from one of the bowls evenly across the crêpe and cook for 2 minutes. Dollop 1 tsp mayonnaise on top and cook for another 10 seconds, then transfer to a large plate. Repeat with the remaining batter until you have 4 filled crêpes. Garnish with basil (or mint) and serve hot.

SHRIMP CAKES
(Tod Mun Goong)
Makes 6 to 8 cakes

½ cup white vinegar

¾ tsp salt

¼ tsp Thai chili sauce

5½ Tbsp white sugar

10 large prawns, rinsed, shelled and deveined

½ tsp potato starch

½ tsp baking powder

1 cup bread crumbs

4 Tbsp vegetable oil

IN A SMALL saucepan, combine vinegar, ¼ tsp of the salt, chili sauce and 5 Tbsp of the sugar. Cook on medium-low heat for 5 to 7 minutes until sugar dissolves completely. Transfer this dipping sauce to a sauce bowl and set aside.

Cut prawns into ½-inch pieces first, then chop and grind them into a paste with a heavy knife or cleaver. Transfer to a medium bowl and add the remaining ½ tsp salt, ½ Tbsp sugar, potato starch and baking powder and mix well.

Lightly dust a clean work surface with cornstarch. Spoon 1 Tbsp of the prawn mixture into one hand and roll it between your palms to a make ball. Press the ball into a ¼-inch-thick round patty and set on the work surface. Repeat with the remaining prawn mixture. You should have 6 to 8 patties.

Place bread crumbs on a large, shallow plate. Dip a patty in the bread crumbs, coating it evenly on both sides and tapping it lightly to remove any excess. Repeat with the remaining patties.

In a large pan, heat vegetable oil on medium-high. Carefully place patties in the pan, leaving a ½ inch around each one. (Pan-fry them in batches, if necessary.) Cook each patty on one side for 3 to 4 minutes, then turn over and cook for another 3 to 4 minutes or until light brown. Serve hot with the dipping sauce on the side.

A DELICIOUS appetizer, snack or street food, these shrimp cakes are thinner than crab cakes, with a smooth, almost firm texture. Although ground prawns or shrimp meat are the key to these cakes, you can also add ground pork or fish to the mix. The spicy vinaigrette served with the patties is a must-have dipping sauce. Adjust the amount of chili sauce to your taste. Although you can make the dipping sauce ahead and refrigerate it in an airtight container for up to one week, the cakes are best enjoyed fresh.

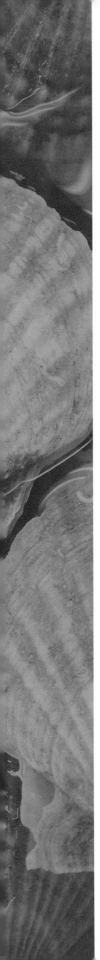

IN ASIA, when it comes to seafood, fresh means caught this morning or still swimming in the live seafood tank! Chefs and home cooks shop at the market very early each day, buying whatever catch has just arrived, then prepare it simply and with little seasoning.

Vancouver's proximity to the Pacific Ocean means that its Asian restaurants can showcase local spot prawns, Dungeness crab and sockeye salmon when they're in season. The city's Chinese seafood restaurants were the first to popularize live seafood on the city's menus, and Sun Sui Wah and Ken's continue to draw crowds for their award-winning maritime dishes, including Steamed Tilapia with Chinese Dried Olives and Preserved Black Bean Sauce.

Vancouver is said to have the best sushi chefs outside Japan, and Tojo's has cemented the city's reputation for exquisitely prepared raw fish sushi and sashimi. And combining their seafood with chilies and curry, Indian and Southeast Asian restaurants turn out fiery but delicious dishes such as Singapore Chili Dungeness Crab. Try a straightforward but delicious Seared Lingcod in a Ponzu and Dashi Broth with Shanghai Bok Choy, or be adventurous and cook up the Steamed Eels and Turnip in Silver Sauce.

SEAFOOD

SOCKEYE SALMON TEMPURA

with Avocado Strips and Japanese Salsa Verde

Serves 2

1 ripe avocado

1 shiso leaf

1 green onion, white and green parts, in ⅛-inch slices

1 oz baby arugula

¼ cup peeled and diced English cucumber

4 Tbsp rice wine vinegar

1 Tbsp shiro (white) soy sauce

5 Tbsp olive oil

2 tsp grated ginger

8 oz fresh sockeye salmon fillet, in 1¼-inch strips

1 tsp sea salt, preferably fleur de sel

one 8-inch square Japanese nori, halved

1 egg yolk

½ cup sifted cake flour

3 cups vegetable oil, for deep-frying

THE DIRTY APRON Cooking School is a non-traditional culinary school that makes cooking fun. From noble French cooking to knife techniques, the school's workshops cover a wide range of subjects. Taking one of the izakaya-style Japanese, Thai classics or other Asian-themed classes could be a delicious and effective way to learn the basics of Asian cookery.

This recipe celebrates the two very popular Japanese staples: sushi and tempura, all in one roll. The pressed avocado strips are a delightful buttery counterpoint to the crispy tempura bites. If you can't find shiso, or Japanese basil, substitute Thai basil. Refrigerate any leftover salsa verde in an airtight container for up to 10 days. Use it as a dipping sauce or a condiment. Serve this dish as an appetizer or a main course.

USING A SHARP knife, cut avocado in half. Remove and discard the pit. Spoon flesh into a small resealable plastic bag and discard the peels. Seal the bag tightly, then, using your hand, mash and spread avocado into a thin even layer that fills the bag. Freeze for 1 hour or until completely solid.

In a food processor, purée shiso, green onions, arugula and cucumber for 45 seconds. Add vinegar and soy sauce and purée for another 45 seconds. Transfer the mixture to a small bowl, then pour in olive oil and whisk for 30 seconds. Add ginger, mix gently and set aside. This is the salsa verde.

Lightly sprinkle salmon with sea salt on both sides. On a clean, dry work surface or a large cutting board, arrange nori with the long edge parallel to the counter. Overlap four slices salmon in a line across each sheet, placing them about 1 inch from the bottom edge of the nori. Tightly fold the bottom edge of the nori over the salmon to envelop it, then continue rolling away from you to form a tight roll. Repeat so that you have two rolls. Cut two large squares of plastic wrap. Set one roll on each sheet of plastic wrap and wrap tightly, twisting the ends to seal them. Refrigerate rolls for about 10 minutes.

In a medium bowl, whisk egg yolk and ice-cold water together, then stir in flour and continue whisking for about 2 minutes, or until the batter is smooth. Set aside.

In a small pot, heat vegetable oil to 325°F. Unwrap the rolls, dip them in the batter, then carefully place them in the oil and blanch for 25 to 30 seconds. Using a slotted spoon, transfer rolls to a wire rack and allow to cool for 2 to 3 minutes.

Remove the bag of avocado from the freezer. Using a sharp knife, cut through the bag to create three equal strips, each 1 inch wide. Remove and discard the plastic bag. Arrange avocado strips on a serving platter as a garnish. Drizzle 1 Tbsp salsa verde over the strips. Cut each roll into 2 to 3 equal pieces and arrange over the salsa. Serve immediately.

ROBSON STREET

HON'S WUN-TUN HOUSE may have been the first Asian noodle house on Robson Street, but thanks to language schools that bring in steady flows of Japanese and Korean students, many hip Japanese and Korean eateries now dominate this trendy downtown street. Benkei Ramen, Kintaro Ramen and Motomachi Shokudo are just a few of the popular ramen restaurants within a few blocks on Robson, and the international ramen chain Hokkaido Ramen Santouka has opened up in the same area, which tells you just how vibrant this West End market is. Probably the best-known eatery of all is Japadog, whose hot dogs loaded with Japanese condiments attracted global attention during the 2010 Vancouver Winter Olympics and have spawned a revolution in the city's street food.

Robson Street is about more than just award-winning Asian fast food. Although the long-lived Gyoza King was the first to wow dinner and late-night crowds with its Japanese tapas, Kobe Japanese Steak and Seafood House on Alberni, just one block north, has been sizzling since 1976. And Aki Japanese Restaurant on Thurlow at Robson, one of the oldest Japanese restaurants in Vancouver, moved from Japantown to lure diners with its classic Japanese fare. A recent trend has seen a huge number of slick new Japanese-style izakayas with ultramodern bars, including the original Hapa Izakaya and Guu Izakaya, on Thurlow, which serves tapas to crowds of local and visiting young hipsters every day and night. Dozens of sushi places (of varying quality) such as Sushi Mart and the all-you-can-eat Robson Sushi have their share of fans, and Chicco Japanese Dessert Cafe also draws a steady stream of sweets lovers for its Japanese-style parfaits.

Korean restaurants, both the traditional barbecue houses and trendy tapas joints, are becoming established on Robson. Ap Gu Jung offers a full soju, wine and drinks list along with its Korean tapas menu; Nor Boo Korean's good and cheap eats remind guests of Mom's home cooking; Book Kyung Ban Jeoum specializes in Korean and Chinese dishes and comforting noodle soups. In the large dining room of Dae Bak Bon Ga, diners can indulge in traditional Korean barbecue meals and classic dishes, while singing karaoke at the same time.

Cheap and cheerful Asian eateries have given Robson Street some visual appeal with their funky façades, and they've given the strip a badly needed injection of fast-food culinary diversity. Also quick and delicious are the growing number of food carts showing up in the downtown core. Reminiscent of the street stalls so popular in Asia, Vancouver's carts feature a number of Asian options. You can spot them from afar, or just let your nose do the navigating: inhale the Asian spices, and you may want two orders of the pork belly at Roaming Dragon (Burrard and Robson). The Vietnamese sub sandwich (bánh mì) from Kiss Kiss Banh Banh (Howe and Robson) is a refreshing and healthy choice. Instead of grabbing a coffee, sip a cup of chai from Chawalla (Howe and Robson); it goes well with all kinds of street food!

WESTVIEW'S HOUSE SPECIAL SPICY PRAWNS

Serves 4

10 oz jumbo prawns, shelled and deveined	1 tsp minced ginger	½ tsp light soy sauce
2 tsp cornstarch	1 tsp minced onion	½ tsp oyster sauce
1 Tbsp canola oil	½ green bell pepper, in ½-inch dice	1 tsp white sugar
1 Tbsp butter	½ red bell pepper, in ½-inch dice	1 tsp sesame oil
1 tsp minced garlic	1 Tbsp chopped fresh cilantro	1 to 2 tsp chili paste

DESPITE THE huge number of Asian restaurants in Metro Vancouver, there are very few on the North Shore. Thank goodness for Westview, which serves both dim sum lunch and a full dinner menu of Cantonese and Szechuanese specialties.

This Mandarin dish combines stir-frying and braising to produce a tangy and spicy seafood entrée. Although this recipe is traditionally made with tiger prawns, Pacific sidestripe shrimp or spot prawns or Nova Scotia trap-caught prawns are good sustainable alternatives. The fully loaded sauce is a welcome dipping sauce for plain steamed buns.

USING A SHARP knife, butterfly prawns by starting at the head and slitting the back all the way to the tail, leaving 1/16-inch of meat still attached. Open the prawns and press down gently. Transfer to a medium bowl, add cornstarch and mix well.

Heat canola oil in a large pan on high, add prawns, cut side down, and brown for 10 seconds. Using a turner, flip prawns over and brown for another 10 seconds. Transfer to a plate.

Reduce the heat to medium. To the same pan, add butter and allow to melt. Stir in garlic, ginger, onions, green and red bell peppers and cilantro, then increase the heat to high and stir-fry for 90 seconds. Add soy sauce, oyster sauce, sugar, sesame oil, chili paste and ¼ cup water, stirring well. Bring to a boil and cook for 3 to 4 minutes. Return prawns to the pan and sauté for 2 to 3 minutes, or until sauce is reduced to the consistency of gravy. Remove from the heat and serve immediately.

PRAWNS IN COCONUT CURRY

Serves 4

2 Tbsp coconut oil	½ onion, sliced	2 lbs prawns, shelled and deveined
1 tsp mustard seeds	1 Tbsp finely chopped ginger	
½ tsp fenugreek seeds	1 tomato, coarsely chopped	2 cups coconut milk
1 tsp cumin seeds	½ tsp turmeric	2 Tbsp chopped fresh cilantro
1 sprig curry leaves	½ tsp chili powder	

HEAT A LARGE pan on medium-high, add coconut oil and heat for 30 seconds. Stir in mustard, fenugreek and cumin seeds. When they start to pop, about 45 seconds, add curry leaves, onions and ginger and sauté for 2 to 3 minutes until onions start to brown. Stir in tomatoes, turmeric and chili powder and sauté for about 5 minutes, or until tomatoes are soft.

Increase the heat to high. Add prawns and salt to taste and cook for 2 to 3 minutes until prawns start to turn reddish. Pour in coconut milk, reduce the heat to medium and simmer for 3 to 4 minutes. Transfer to a deep serving dish and garnish with cilantro. Serve immediately.

CHUTNEY VILLA is one of the few places in Vancouver to find South Indian food. The *New York Times* has praised its breads (dosas, uttappams and murtabak) and, not surprisingly, its condiments (chutneys, sambars and raita). Try its delicious masala dosa.

The best place to buy coconut oil, coconut milk or any other coconut products for Indian cooking is in South Asian markets. The same goes for fresh vegetables, herbs and spices, such as sprigs of curry leaves, onions and tomatoes. Serve this dish with basmati rice or roti.

SINGAPORE CHILI DUNGENESS CRAB

Serves 2

1 fresh Dungeness crab, 2½ lbs

6 cups vegetable oil, for deep-frying

3 Tbsp canola oil

10 cloves garlic, finely chopped

1 Tbsp chopped ginger

3 red hot chili peppers, finely chopped

1 Tbsp chili sauce

½ cup tomato sauce

1 Tbsp white sugar

1 Tbsp light soy sauce

1 Tbsp sesame oil

1 cup chicken stock

1 Tbsp cornstarch

1 egg, lightly beaten

1 green onion, in ⅛-inch dice

ASIANS LOVE to buy crab fresh and whole, and cook everything including the shell, so that no meat is lost and the dish looks spectacular when served. In fact, many seafood lovers crave deep-fried crab tomalley still in the shell.

HOLDING THE CRAB'S body in one hand, hook your thumb under the front of the shell and pull hard. The shell should pop off. Gently rinse the contents but leave them intact. Using a cutting board and a cleaver, clean and chop the rest of the crab into 6 to 8 pieces and set it aside with the shell.

Line a large plate with paper towels. In a wok or a deep fryer, bring vegetable oil to 350°F. Add crab shell and pieces and cook for 3 to 5 minutes, or until bright red. Using tongs, transfer crab to the paper towel–lined plate to drain.

In another wok, heat canola oil on high. Add garlic, ginger and chili peppers and sauté for 30 seconds. Stir in chili sauce, tomato sauce, sugar, soy sauce and sesame oil, mix well and bring to a boil. Stir in crab pieces and the shell, then slowly pour in chicken stock and sauté for 2 minutes.

In a small bowl, beat cornstarch with 3 Tbsp water and egg until creamy, then slowly pour into the wok. Stir and cook for another 1 minute and turn off the heat. Garnish with green onions and serve hot on a platter, family-style.

Scallops Stuffed with Chinese Ham (page 102) >

SCALLOPS STUFFED WITH CHINESE HAM

Serves 4

12 large scallops	2 Tbsp liquid honey	1 cup + 2 tsp canola oil
1 tsp sea salt	two 2-inch-long celery stalks, julienned in 12 even pieces	4 oz broccoli, in 12 florets
½ tsp freshly ground black pepper		4 tsp cornstarch
½ tsp sesame oil	one 2-inch-long carrot, julienned in 12 even pieces	2 Tbsp chicken broth
1 oz Chinese ham, in twelve ¼- × 2-inch lengths		

THIS SCALLOP dish is one of Jade Dynasty's award-winning signature recipes created by Chef Lee. He also oversees the restaurant's dim sum menu and created the much-lauded nutty taro roll, a dessert. The restaurant consistently wins accolades for its seafood, too.

Yunnan ham, the whole hind leg salted, cured and hung to dry like Italian prosciutto, is the finest and most expensive Chinese ham. Each bite carries both a hint of honey and smoked salt, and the taste is so ambrosial that a little goes a long way. It's an essential ingredient in premium soup stocks and certain delicacies; if you can't find it, use salted Chinese-style ham. At the restaurant, Chef Lee garnishes this dish with unstuffed marinated scallops, lightly breaded and deep fried.

IN A SMALL bowl, gently mix scallops with ½ tsp of the sea salt, black pepper and sesame oil. Set aside for at least 20 minutes.

In a wok or a large saucepan, bring 2 cups water to a boil on high heat. Set a bamboo steamer or a steamer insert in the wok or saucepan. Arrange ham in a heatproof dish small enough to fit in the steamer and drizzle with honey. Place the dish in the steamer and steam for 20 minutes. Remove and set aside.

Using a sharp knife, make a ¼-inch slit in the middle of a scallop. Fill the incision with one slice of ham, a piece of celery and a piece of carrot. Repeat with the remaining scallops and fillings, then arrange scallops in a deep heatproof dish.

Line a plate with paper towels. In a medium saucepan, carefully bring 1 cup canola oil to a full boil on medium-high heat. Slowly and evenly pour hot oil over scallops to parcook them. Using a slotted spoon, transfer scallops to the paper towel–lined plate to drain and set aside. Allow the oil to cool completely and reserve for another use.

In another medium saucepan, bring 2 cups water to a boil on high heat. Add the remaining ½ tsp sea salt, 1 tsp of the canola oil and broccoli. Cover and cook for 90 seconds, then remove from the heat and drain.

In a small bowl, mix cornstarch and 2 Tbsp water until well combined. Heat a wok on high heat and add the remaining 1 tsp canola oil. Place parcooked scallops in the wok, pour in chicken broth and cook for 1 minute. Gently add the cornstarch mixture and cook for another 15 to 20 seconds until it starts to boil. Turn off the heat.

Place stuffed scallops on a large serving platter, arrange broccoli florets around the scallops and serve hot.

SAUTÉED SCALLOPS AND CHICKEN
with Broccoli and Crispy Milk Fritters

Serves 4 to 6

CRISPY MILK FRITTERS	
½ cup homogenized milk	4 cups canola oil, for deep-frying
2 Tbsp cornstarch	3 Tbsp all-purpose flour
2 Tbsp white sugar	2 tsp baking powder
	1 Tbsp vegetable oil

DAIRY PRODUCTS rarely make their way to Chinese dinner tables, except for a dish called "milk fritters." The original fritters were made from the milk of buffalo cows raised in Daliang, a county in Guangdong Province, but their popularity has spread far and wide. Use your own locally produced milk to make these battered and deep-fried crispy fritters. Allow at least 2 hours to refrigerate the batter before you make them.

CRISPY MILK FRITTERS Have ready a 6-inch square glass or ceramic container with a lid. Pour milk, cornstarch, sugar and ½ cup cold water into a medium saucepan, stir and bring to a boil on medium heat. Remove from the heat, transfer to the container and allow to rest for 15 minutes. Cover and refrigerate for at least 2 hours, or until the mixture sets like gelatin. (If a toothpick inserted in the mixture comes out clean, the milk gelatin is ready for deep-frying.)

In a wok or a deep fryer, heat canola oil to 350°F.

In a medium bowl, whisk together flour, baking powder, vegetable oil and 6 Tbsp water until well combined.

Line a wire rack with paper towels. Using a sharp knife, cut milk gelatin into 1- × 2-inch pieces. (You should have 18 pieces.) Dip each piece into the batter, then deep-fry for about 1 minute, or until golden brown. Using a slotted spoon, transfer fritters to the rack to drain. Set aside.

**SAUTÉED SCALLOPS
AND CHICKEN**

2 Tbsp vegetable oil

1 tsp chopped garlic

10 oz broccoli florets

5 oz chicken breast, sliced

3 scallops, halved horizontally

½ green bell pepper, sliced

½ red bell pepper, sliced

½ tsp fish sauce

½ tsp chili bean paste

½ tsp white sugar

½ tsp oyster sauce

1 Tbsp cornstarch

SAUTÉED SCALLOPS AND CHICKEN   Heat a wok on high. Add 1 Tbsp of the vegetable oil and ½ tsp of the garlic. Stir in broccoli and sauté for 15 seconds. Add 2 Tbsp water, cover and cook for 45 seconds. Transfer to a 10-inch round dish and set aside.

Add the remaining 1 Tbsp vegetable oil and ½ tsp garlic to the wok and bring to a sizzle. Add chicken and scallops and sauté for 90 seconds. Stir in green and red bell peppers and mix well. Add fish sauce, chili bean paste, sugar and oyster sauce, stir for 10 seconds, then cover and cook for 1 minute. Remove the cover.

In a small bowl, mix cornstarch with 2 Tbsp water until well combined. Slowly pour this mixture into the wok and sauté for 15 seconds. Turn off the heat and spoon the chili-prawn mixture over the broccoli. Scatter milk fritters around the edge and serve immediately.

SEA URCHIN AND SCALLOP MOUSSE
with Umami Jelly and Watercress-Daikon Salad

Serves 4

2 fresh Qualicum Bay scallops, chilled	6 leaves gelatin or 3 tsp gelatin powder	Small handful of bonito flakes
3½ oz fresh red sea urchin roe	½ cup ponzu sauce	2 Tbsp chopped watercress
3 egg whites	½ cup whipped cream	2 Tbsp julienned daikon
1½ cups whipping cream	one 2-inch piece of kombu	1 tsp extra-virgin olive oil
Pinch of cayenne pepper	2 dried shiitake mushrooms	4 nori rice crackers

RED SEA urchin is a favourite of sushi lovers who rave about its bittersweet ambrosial flavour and velvety texture. Here it's paired with sweet, succulent and naturally large scallops from Qualicum Bay, in a delicious appetizer that conjoins the culinary arts of Europe and Japan. Blue Water Cafe was the first restaurant in B.C. to open a state-of-the-art raw bar. The restaurant's focus on local, sustainable seafood has garnered it many awards and the respect of diners and critics across the country.

Red sea urchin roe and Qualicum Bay scallops are available in specialty seafood stores. Prepare the mousse the night before you plan to serve it.

HAVE READY AN 8- × 4-inch (4-cup) loaf pan and a large stockpot.

In a blender, purée scallops, sea urchin and egg whites until very smooth. Add whipping cream and pulse for 15 seconds. Set a fine-mesh sieve over a clean bowl and strain the seafood mixture through it, discarding the excess liquid that collects in the bowl. This step helps to condense and smooth the mixture. Season with a pinch of salt and cayenne pepper. Using a spatula, spoon the mixture into the loaf pan and cover tightly with aluminum foil.

Fill the stockpot with 1½ inches water. Be sure the water does not extend any higher than three-quarters of the way up the loaf pan. Heat water on medium, then as soon as the water begins to boil, reduce the heat to a simmer. Set the loaf pan in the water and poach seafood for 20 minutes, or until set and a metal skewer inserted in the centre is warm to the touch.

Using tongs, remove the loaf pan from the stockpot. Allow to cool on a wire rack for 10 minutes, then refrigerate overnight or for at least 12 hours.

Three hours before serving time, scrape the seafood mixture into a blender. Mix for 3 to 5 minutes, or until very smooth and mousse-like. Transfer to a large bowl.

If using gelatin leaves, fill a small bowl with 1 cup cold water. Add 3 leaves and allow to bloom for 10 minutes. Rinse gelatin and squeeze out any excess water. Set aside.

In a medium microwave-safe bowl, microwave ponzu sauce on high heat for 15 seconds. Add bloomed gelatin leaves or 1½ tsp gelatin powder and stir for 90 seconds or until dissolved. Using a spatula, fold the gelatin mixture into the seafood mousse until well mixed. Gently fold in whipped cream until combined. Divide mousse among 4 glass bowls (or martini glasses) and refrigerate for at least 2 hours.

While the mousse is setting, prepare umami jelly. In a small pot, bring ½ cup water, kombu and shiitake mushrooms to a simmer on medium heat. Turn off the heat. Using a pair of tongs, remove and discard kombu. Stir in bonito flakes and allow to infuse for 10 minutes.

Place a fine-mesh sieve over a clean bowl. Pour infusion through the sieve, discarding any solids. Set aside this broth.

If using gelatin leaves, fill a small bowl with 1 cup cold water. Add 3 leaves and allow to bloom for 10 minutes. Rinse gelatin and squeeze out any excess water. Add bloomed gelatin leaves or 1½ tsp gelatin powder to broth and stir for 90 seconds or until dissolved. Pour this mixture into a small loaf pan, cover and refrigerate for at 2 hours.

Just before serving, remove mousse and jelly from the refrigerator. Evenly cut jelly into 4 portions and garnish each mousse.

In a medium bowl, combine watercress and daikon. Add olive oil and toss well. Using tongs, garnish each mousse with some salad, then top with a nori cracker. Serve immediately.

Daikon

IN RECENT YEARS, the area around the Joyce SkyTrain Station has seen an increase in Filipino stores and restaurants. Before then, Fraser and Main Streets held the greatest concentration, and they are still home to some of the best. Pinpin Restaurant consistently tops the list for its homemade Filipino-Chinese food, and it has drawn a number of bakeries and convenience stores to the area around Fraser near 45th Avenue. On Main, Josephine's was one of the first Filipino restaurants in East Vancouver, and it has been joined by Goldilocks Bakery and Aling Mary's store, which stocks such favourite Filipino staples as cane vinegar, banana catsup and packages of dried gabi (taro leaves). At any of the restaurants, try the mixed vegetables and adobo chicken, which are perennial favourites.

The re-energized community around Joyce Street is anchored by two family-operated Filipino restaurants located side by side in the same strip mall: Cucina Manila, which serves home-style Filipino food, and Goto King, which lures diners in with Chinese-Filipino food. Both cafeteria-style eateries feature an array of hot foods, including deep-fried fish, fried chicken and snacks. Try the daily specials, which might feature deep-fried roasted pork, braised pig feet and/or pork blood.

Pockets of Filipino markets and restaurants are also popping up in other neighbourhoods such as North Vancouver, Richmond, Surrey and Burnaby. They are often a gathering place for Filipinos and Filipino-Chinese, and you're likely to find yourself seated beside groups of women, with their kids, catching up with friends. For many Filipino women who have left their husbands and sometimes their children to work as housekeepers and nannies in Canada, these restaurants are their chance to relax, meet up with other Filipino "family" and enjoy the taste of home.

The best-kept Filipino foodie secret in the region? Kulinarya Restaurant in Coquitlam.

STEAMED TILAPIA WITH CHINESE DRIED OLIVES
and Preserved Black Bean Sauce

Serves 4

1½ lbs whole fresh tilapia, cleaned and patted dry

6 Chinese dried black olives, chopped

2 tsp fermented black beans, rinsed and chopped

1 tsp finely chopped ginger

1 tsp white sugar

2 tsp light soy sauce

½ tsp dark soy sauce

1 tsp cornstarch

4 Tbsp canola oil

1 green onion, julienned

USING A SHARP, heavy knife, slice gently along tilapia's backbone to separate the fish into 2 fillets, then chop the flesh into 2-inch lengths. You should have 6 to 8 pieces in total. Arrange tilapia strips, skin side down, on a large plate. (Asians traditionally keep the head and tail and cook these along with the body, but discard them if you prefer.) Discard the bones (or reserve them to make fish stock).

In a small bowl, combine olives, black beans, ginger, sugar, light and dark soy sauces, cornstarch and 1 Tbsp of the canola oil. Using a spoon, spread the mixture evenly over the tilapia. Transfer the plate of tilapia to a bamboo steamer.

In a large wok, bring 2 cups water to a boil on high heat, set steamer on top (make sure the water is boiling), cover and steam for 10 minutes. Remove from the heat and set aside.

In a small saucepan, bring remaining 3 Tbsp canola oil to a boil on high heat. Carefully pour hot oil evenly over fish, garnish with green onions and serve immediately.

ALONG THE southeast coast of China, eating steamed freshly caught seafood is a way of life. Most commonly it is flavoured with shredded fresh ginger and green onions, but others prefer sun-dried vegetables, smoked ham, dried mushrooms, chili and garlic sauce or, as in this recipe, dried olives and black bean sauce.

Pouring hot oil over the tilapia is an integral part of this recipe, as it merges with the juices obtained from steaming the fish and the seasoning ingredients to create a fish sauce with an umami flavour. Even if you're watching your fat intake, don't skip this step!

This version comes courtesy of Chef Liang, whose award-winning golden Dungeness crab (cooked with preserved egg yolks) and lobster hot pot (cooked with ginger and mung bean threads) regularly draw diners from Toronto and New York.

SEARED LINGCOD IN A PONZU AND DASHI BROTH
with Shanghai Bok Choy

Serves 4

DASHI

one 2-inch square kombu

¼ cup shaved dry bonito flakes

SEARED LINGCOD WITH SHANGHAI BOK CHOY

3 Tbsp canola oil

4 lingcod fillets, each 5 oz

2 tsp salt

2 Tbsp unsalted butter

¼ cup + 1 Tbsp ponzu sauce

1 Tbsp mirin

20 whole baby Shanghai bok choy, rinsed and drained

CHINESE ENJOY fish soup and, very often, devour the flesh by dipping it in chilies and soy sauce. Firm textured, flaky and mild flavoured, lingcod is the perfect fish for soups. This clean-tasting, flavourful dish showcases Chef Peckham's French culinary training and her interest in local, seasonal products, trademarks that have brought particular attention to her small-plates menu at Cru Restaurant.

Dashi is best used the same day, but any leftover broth can be refrigerated in an airtight container for up to 2 days and used as a soup base or dipping sauce.

DASHI Place 4 cups water and kombu in a medium saucepan and bring to a boil on high heat. Immediately reduce the heat to low and simmer for 30 minutes. Remove kombu and turn off the heat. Add bonito flakes and allow to steep for 30 minutes. Place a fine-mesh sieve over a medium saucepan. Strain broth, discarding bonito flakes and any other solids.

LINGCOD Preheat the oven to 475°F.

In a large ovenproof pan, heat canola oil on high. Sprinkle lingcod with 1 tsp of the salt. When the pan is hot and smoking, gently place lingcod in the pan and cook until the edges are golden brown, 2 to 3 minutes. Place the pan in the oven and grill for 3 to 5 minutes, until fish is cooked and flakes when poked with a fork. Remove the pan from the oven.

Gently turn fish over, add butter and 1 Tbsp ponzu sauce and allow to sizzle until butter melts completely. Set aside.

Place the saucepan of dashi on high heat, add mirin, the remaining 1 tsp salt, ¼ cup ponzu sauce and bring to a boil. Add bok choy and cook for 45 seconds. To serve, arrange 1 piece of lingcod and 5 pieces of bok choy on each of 4 plates. Drizzle each serving with ¼ cup of the dashi sauce and serve immediately.

PAN-GRILLED SALMON STEAKS
with Chili Bean Sauce and Chinese Wine Kasu
Serves 4

2 pink or chum salmon steaks, each 6 oz, skin on

3 Tbsp chili bean sauce

½ tsp freshly ground black pepper

2 Tbsp canola oil

1 slice ginger, skin on

2 cloves garlic, finely chopped

1 tsp tomato paste

1 Tbsp white sugar

1 Tbsp Chinese rice wine kasu

1 tsp cornstarch

½ tsp sesame oil

1 tsp black rice vinegar

1 green onion, in ¼-inch dice

USING A SPOON, evenly spread 1 Tbsp chili bean sauce over salmon steaks, coating both sides. Season with black pepper and set aside for 10 minutes to allow the flavours to infuse.

In a wok, heat canola oil on high. Carefully add salmon and brown for 2 minutes, then turn over and sear for another 2 minutes. Using a slotted spoon, transfer fish to a large plate.

To the wok, add ginger, garlic, the remaining 2 Tbsp chili bean sauce and 6 Tbsp water and cook for 10 seconds. Add salmon to wok, cover and cook for 3 minutes.

In a small bowl, combine tomato paste, sugar and kasu until well mixed, then add to the wok. In the same bowl, combine 2 Tbsp water and cornstarch and pour into the wok. Stir in sesame oil, vinegar and green onions and cook until sizzling, about 30 seconds. Transfer to a platter and serve hot, family-style.

DELICIOUS CUISINE is a trendy Richmond restaurant in the city centre that's the epitome of the new contemporary Taiwanese café popping up all over Metro Vancouver. Run by a father-and-son team, the café is known not only for creative bubble teas and other beverages but also for traditional Taiwanese snacks and lunch and dinner dishes as well as for West Coast–influenced fare.

Both the chili bean sauce and kasu are essential seasonings in many Taiwanese and northern Chinese regions. Bean sauce, which is made from fermented soy beans, can be sweet, mild or hot. Kasu, Chinese distilled rice wine lees, is used in soups, entrées and, most commonly, in desserts. Look for it in plastic containers in the cooler section of Asian supermarkets. Serve this dish with bowls of steamed Japanese rice.

STEAMED EELS AND TURNIP
in Silver Sauce

Serves 4

10 oz turnip, peeled, grated and squeezed dry	4 oz freshwater or saltwater eel, in four ¾-inch cubes	2 Tbsp mirin
1 egg white	4 B.C. spot prawns, peeled and deveined	2 Tbsp white sugar
¼ tsp sea salt		2 Tbsp light soy sauce
2 oz oyster mushrooms, julienned	8 ginkgo nuts	3 tsp cornstarch
¼ bunch mitsuba	1¼ cups dashi (page 110)	Wasabi paste to taste

THE FIFTEEN-YEAR-OLD Pacific Institute of Culinary Arts (PICA) is an award-winning culinary school that provides certified professional training programs in classic French and international cuisine, as well as short courses for recreational cooks. A graduate of the esteemed Japan Cooking School in Osaka, as well as kitchens in both Toronto and Montreal, Chef Inoue is one of the school's chef instructors.

Raw eel is available in the frozen seafood section of Asian markets. Thaw the fish in the refrigerator overnight. To remove the spine bone, use a sharp knife to make a horizontal cut right above the spine, turn the fish over and repeat the same cut. Discard the bony middle piece and work with the two filets of eel. There's no need to remove any other bones, as they are tender and chewy. If you can't find, or don't want to eat eel, substitute sablefish or swordfish.

In Japanese cooking, *gin-an*, or silver sauce, is the one most associated with steamed fish. It's made by thickening dashi with cornstarch.

IN A MEDIUM bowl, combine turnip and egg white and season with sea salt. Add mushrooms and mitsuba and toss well. Evenly divide this mixture among 4 small, ceramic Japanese miso soup bowls. Add 1 piece of eel, 1 spot prawn and 2 ginkgo nuts to each bowl.

In a wok fitted with a bamboo steamer or in a covered steamer, bring 6 cups water to a boil on high heat. Turn down the heat to medium. Arrange the bowls in the bamboo steamer or steamer insert, cover with a lid or aluminum foil and steam for 10 minutes. Remove from the heat and set aside.

In a medium saucepan, combine dashi, mirin, sugar and soy sauce and bring to a boil on medium-high heat.

In a small bowl, combine cornstarch and 3 tsp water until it forms a smooth paste. Slowly add the mixture to the saucepan and stir gently for 10 to 15 seconds until the sauce thickens. Evenly divide silver sauce among the 4 bowls. Garnish with wasabi and serve hot.

Spicy Vietnamese Seafood Hot Pot (Lau Thai) (page 114) >

SPICY VIETNAMESE SEAFOOD HOT POT
(Lau Thai)
Serves 6 to 8

SPICE SACHET

2 stalks lemon grass, bulb
part only, crushed

3 kaffir lime leaves

4 to 6 sprigs fresh Thai basil

4 to 6 sprigs fresh cilantro

1 tsp chrysanthemum leaves

3 whole star anise

12 white peppercorns

ALTHOUGH CHEF Dang grew up in Alberta and has trained with some of North America's master chefs, including David Hawksworth and Robert Clark, his Vietnamese heritage serves as the backbone for his creativity. This classic lau Thai is one of the dishes he enjoys with friends and family.

Hot pot is a fondue-style meal. In this version, succulent fresh seafood is dipped in an intensely flavoured, spicy Vietnamese broth. To make this recipe, you'll need a tabletop butane stove and a 3½-inch-high stainless steel Chinese fondue pot, both of which are available at Asian supermarkets. Prepare the broth 90 minutes in advance of the meal to allow it some time to simmer, and start to soak the rice noodles about 45 minutes ahead of mealtime. Look for chrysanthemum leaves and Vietnamese fish balls in any Asian supermarket.

SPICE SACHET Make a spice sachet by placing a 6-inch square piece of cheesecloth on a clean work surface. Arrange lemon grass, lime leaves, Thai basil, cilantro, chrysanthemum leaves, star anise and peppercorns in the middle of the cheesecloth. Gather the corners of the cheesecloth, completely encasing the spices, and tie tightly with a piece of kitchen twine.

HOT POT

4 cups chicken stock

1 cup + 4 Tbsp fish sauce

2 Tbsp light soy sauce

3 Tbsp cane sugar

6 Thai bird's eye chili peppers, halved lengthwise

8 cloves garlic, peeled

two ¼-inch pieces ginger, sliced

2 tomatoes, in 1-inch dice

½ fresh pineapple, peeled and cored, in 1-inch dice

8 white crimini mushrooms, quartered

1 pkg (454 g) Vietnamese dried vermicelli (rice stick)

4 Tbsp chili oil

4 Tbsp fresh lime juice

1 bunch water spinach, rinsed, drained and roughly torn

1 bunch watercress, rinsed and drained

2 bunches regular spinach, rinsed and drained

1 lb squid tubes, in ½-inch rings

1 sablefish fillet, about 2 lbs, thinly sliced

2 lbs spot prawns, heads removed

1 lb scallops, thinly sliced

2 lbs mussels, steamed for 3 minutes then chilled

1 lb Vietnamese fish balls

2 lbs Dungeness crab legs

HOT POT In a medium stockpot, combine chicken stock, 1 cup fish sauce, soy sauce, sugar, chili peppers, garlic, ginger, tomatoes, pineapple, mushrooms and the spice sachet and bring to a boil on high heat. Reduce the heat to low, cover and simmer for at least 90 minutes.

While the broth is simmering, and 45 minutes before you plan to serve the hot pot, place 10 cups water in a large bowl or a saucepan. Add rice noodles and soak for 30 minutes. Drain in a colander for 15 minutes. Transfer vermicelli to a large bowl and set aside.

To make a dipping sauce, combine chili oil, 4 Tbsp fish sauce and lime juice in a small bowl. Pour into a sauce bowl or serve in individual dipping bowls.

To serve, arrange vermicelli, water spinach, watercress, spinach, squid, sablefish, prawns, scallops, mussels, fish balls and crab legs in individual serving bowls and place on the dining table.

Set up the butane stove in the middle of the table. Remove and discard the spice sachet from the broth, then pour it into the hot pot, filling it to within 1 inch from the rim. Set the hot pot on the butane stove on high heat and bring to a full boil. Provide each guest with a plate, a bowl and a set of chopsticks (or a fork) and start dipping seafood and vegetables in the broth for several minutes until cooked. Serve with the dipping sauce. As the broth evaporates, add water as required.

FOR MANY people, one of the most striking things about a walk through an Asian market is the sight of chicken feet and whole ducks spilling from boxes in shop stalls. History tells us that China was the first country to breed chickens for food, followed by ducks, squabs and quails, so it's not surprising to find an extended list of Chinese poultry recipes. Be prepared to see both the head and the tail of the bird attached when ordering dishes in a Chinese restaurant. Chicken is also favoured in India, where it's turned into the famous butter chicken, tandoori chicken, chicken tikka and curry chicken dishes.

Asians don't often cook with turkey, but duck is popular in China, Singapore, Indonesia, Thailand and Vietnam. Try the Red Curry Duck. Around Vancouver, several Fraser Valley farms are raising free-range chickens, whose clean flavour is perfect for such dishes as Vietnamese Grilled Chicken with Lemon Grass and Chicken and Three Mushrooms in a Pouch. If you can find them, try silkies, a special breed of chicken favoured in China that has charcoal-coloured skin, dark meat and fluffy white feathers that are silky soft to the touch. Or try quails and squabs, which have their own succulent flavour.

POULTRY

TAIWANESE FIVE-SPICE CHICKEN NUGGETS

Serves 3 to 4

1½ lbs chicken thigh meat, in ¼-inch-thick nuggets	½ tsp freshly ground white pepper	4 cups vegetable oil, for deep-frying
2 Tbsp dark soy sauce	½ tsp five-spice powder	1 cup yam flour
2 tsp white sugar	2 tsp minced garlic	4 to 5 fresh basil leaves, chopped
	1 Tbsp potato starch	

THE CHINESE name of the very stylish Zephyr Tea House Café is "Aroma," which perfectly describes the fragrances that waft through the café from the colourful drinks and bubble teas and the extensive menu of appetizers and side dishes, hot pots and noodles and soups.

Chicken nuggets may not sound like Asian food, but these toothsome morsels pair beautifully with bubble tea and are one of the main meat entrées on the menu in almost every Taiwanese eatery. Dusted with yam flour (which is available in 300-gram packages at Asian markets) then quickly blanched in oil, these flavourful nuggets are crispy on the outside, chewy and tender inside. Start this recipe the day before you plan to serve it, as the nuggets need to marinate overnight.

IN A MEDIUM bowl, toss chicken with soy sauce, sugar, white pepper, five-spice powder, garlic and potato starch until well combined. Cover and refrigerate overnight.

Line a large plate with paper towels. In a medium saucepan or a deep fryer, heat vegetable oil to 330°F. Place yam flour in a deep dish. Dip chicken nuggets in the flour, roll them around until evenly coated, then lightly tap them to remove any excess flour. Carefully place nuggets in the oil and cook for 5 to 6 minutes, or until light brown. Using a slotted spoon, transfer chicken to the paper towel–lined plate to drain. (Alternatively, bake the nuggets in a preheated 375°F oven. Line a baking sheet with parchment paper, spread the nuggets evenly on the paper and bake for 20 to 25 minutes. Increase the heat to broil and cook for 2 to 3 minutes more until the chicken is yellow-orange.) Allow to cool for 2 to 3 minutes, then garnish with basil and serve immediately.

BEIJING-STYLE CHICKEN TENDERS

Serves 4

3 cups vegetable oil, for deep-frying	1 egg, beaten	1 Tbsp Maggi sauce
½ cup all-purpose flour	2 Tbsp white sugar	1 Tbsp red rice vinegar
8 oz chicken thigh meat, in ⅛-inch slices	1 Tbsp HP sauce	½ tsp white sesame seeds
¾ tsp salt	1 Tbsp ketchup	
	1 Tbsp hoisin sauce	

IN A LARGE saucepan or a deep fryer, heat vegetable oil to 325°F.

Line a large plate with paper towels. Place flour on a large, shallow plate. In a large bowl, combine chicken, ¼ tsp of the salt and egg until well coated. Lightly dip chicken pieces in flour to coat, shaking off any excess, then carefully place in oil and blanch for 2 to 3 minutes, or until golden. Using a slotted spoon, transfer the chicken to the paper towel–lined plate to drain.

To make the Beijing sauce, combine sugar, the remaining ½ tsp salt, HP sauce, ketchup, hoisin sauce, Maggi sauce and vinegar in a small saucepan. Bring to a boil on medium heat, then reduce the heat to low, cover and simmer for 2 minutes. Remove from the heat.

Place a wok on high heat. Add chicken and sauté for 30 seconds, then slowly drizzle in the Beijing sauce and stir-fry for 2 minutes. Sprinkle with sesame seeds and serve hot, family-style.

THE APPLICATION of sassy Beijing sauce makes these nuggets a very popular Mandarin chicken dish, which can be served as an appetizer or an entrée. This sweet-and-sour sauce made using Western ingredients such as ketchup and HP sauce is often used in other meat or seafood recipes such as pork chops and fish nuggets. If you like, use hot chili peppers or chili sauce to add heat to this dish.

SHAMI (SPICY CHICKEN) KEBABS

Serves 4

4 whole cloves

1-inch cinnamon stick, crushed

1 whole pod black cardamom

1 tsp cumin seeds

2 lbs raw chicken meat, minced

1 small onion, chopped

¼ tsp freshly ground black pepper

1 tsp chopped garlic

1 tsp chopped ginger

1 green chili pepper, seeded and chopped

¼ cup coarsely chopped fresh cilantro leaves

1 egg, beaten

¼ cup bread crumbs

ASHIANA, WHICH opened in 1980, is one of Vancouver's few long-standing Indian restaurants. Its clay tandoor oven, heated by red-hot charcoal, turns out superlative naan and other tandoori dishes.

Easier for home cooks to make are these patty-style kebabs, popular snacks and appetizers in India, Pakistan and Afghanistan. The spicy minced-meat patties are made with chicken, lamb or beef, whereas chickpeas are the most common ingredient for vegetarian kebabs. Enjoy them, served on wooden skewers, with mint or tamarind chutney. You can refrigerate leftover kebabs in an airtight container for a day or two.

PREHEAT THE OVEN to 350°F. Lightly grease a large baking sheet.

In a food processor or a spice/coffee grinder, grind cloves, cinnamon and cardamom to a fine powder.

Place cumin seeds in a small heatproof dish and roast in the oven for 1 to 2 minutes until light brown and fragrant. Remove from the oven and allow to cool. Leave the oven on.

In a medium bowl, combine spice powder mixture, cumin, chicken, onion, black pepper, garlic, ginger, chili pepper, cilantro and egg. Using a fork, mix well for 2 to 3 minutes or until the mixture is uniform and holds together. Add bread crumbs and blend gently for another minute.

Using your hands, scoop a small handful of the chicken mixture into your palm. Roll it into a log about 3 inches long by 1 inch around. Place kebab on the baking sheet, leaving at least 1 inch around all sides. Repeat with the remaining chicken mixture. You should have about 8 kebabs. Bake kebabs for 15 minutes, then turn them over and bake for another 10 minutes, or until golden brown. Allow to cool for 5 minutes before serving.

CHICKEN AND THREE MUSHROOMS IN A POUCH

Serves 4

4 oz chicken thigh meat, in ½-inch strips	1 oz fresh king oyster mushrooms, julienned	1 Tbsp rice vinegar
½ tsp salt	1 slice lemon, quartered	1 Tbsp fresh lemon juice
½ tsp freshly ground black pepper	2 tsp butter	¼ tsp mirin
1 oz fresh enoki mushrooms	1 tsp sake	2 Tbsp chopped green onions, white and green parts
1 fresh medium shiitake mushroom, julienned	1 Tbsp + 1 tsp Japanese soy sauce (shoyu)	

JULIENNES OF chicken and three kinds of fresh mushrooms are steamed in a simple yet exquisite sauce. The result is presented in the shape of a pouch and is indeed a sublime gift of an appetizer. This is an example of one of Chef Omori's traditional dishes presented izakaya-style.

To make this dish, you will need four sheets of parchment paper, each cut into an 8-inch square, plus four pieces of kitchen twine. Have these ready before you begin cooking.

IN A MEDIUM bowl, sprinkle chicken with salt and black pepper.

Trim and discard 1½ inches from the bottom of enoki mushrooms and separate them by hand. Cut into 1-inch lengths.

Place squares of parchment paper on a clean, dry work surface. Evenly divide chicken, enoki, shiitake and king oyster mushrooms, lemon slices, butter, sake and 1 tsp soy sauce among the four parchment squares. Gather the corners of one parchment paper, completely encasing the filling, and tie tightly with a piece of kitchen twine. Repeat with the remaining parchment squares.

In a wok fitted with a bamboo steamer or in a covered steamer, bring 2 cups water to a boil on high heat. Arrange the parchment packages in the steamer, uncovered, and steam for 20 minutes.

While the packages are steaming, make the ponzu sauce. In a small bowl, combine vinegar, lemon juice, 1 Tbsp soy sauce, mirin and green onions. Divide the sauce among 4 dipping bowls.

To serve, place a parchment pouch on each of 4 individual plates. Using a pair of scissors, cut the twine. Warn diners to be careful when untying the kitchen twine, as the pouches will release very hot steam. Serve immediately with a small soup spoon and individual bowls of ponzu sauce.

CHICKEN À LA KING

Serves 2

6 oz chicken breast, sliced	3 Tbsp butter	2 Tbsp white wine
1 tsp light soy sauce	4 medium crimini mushrooms, quartered	½ cup chicken stock
1 tsp white sugar		2 Tbsp all-purpose flour
1 Tbsp cornstarch	½ red bell pepper, sliced	2 Tbsp mayonnaise
1 Tbsp canola oil	1 small onion, in ½-inch slices	½ cup half-and-half cream

IN A MEDIUM bowl, toss chicken with soy sauce, ½ tsp of the sugar, cornstarch and a pinch of salt and set aside for at least 15 minutes.

In a wok, heat canola oil on high, add chicken and marinade, and stir and cook for 2 minutes. Transfer chicken to a large bowl. Reduce the heat to medium.

To the wok, add 1 Tbsp butter and allow it to melt. Add mushrooms, bell peppers and onions and sauté for 1 minute. Increase the heat to medium-high and stir in chicken. Cover and cook for 2 minutes, then transfer all ingredients back to the bowl. Reduce the heat to medium.

To the wok, add the remaining 2 Tbsp butter and allow it to melt. Slowly pour in wine and chicken stock and bring to a low boil. Gently stir in the remaining ½ tsp sugar, flour, mayonnaise and cream. Return chicken and vegetables to the wok, increase the heat to high and sauté for 30 seconds. Serve hot on individual plates.

A DISH of diced ingredients, butter and cream said to have originated in New York, chicken à la King is regarded as one of the earliest "East meets West" creations and is served on individual plates. It was very popular in chop-suey cafés and at Chinese smorgasbord buffet counters across North America until the mid-eighties. It then made its way to Hong Kong–style cafés in Asia, where à la King recipes incorporating other meat and seafood ingredients have flourished. This authentic version from one of the city's newest Asian-meets-Western cafés is a nod to times past. Serve this dish over steamed rice or pasta.

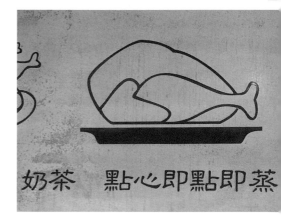

SPICY CHICKEN
with Ginger and Black Beans
Serves 3 to 4

2 Tbsp canola oil	1 small onion, julienned	1 Tbsp tomato paste
1 lb chicken thighs, in 1-inch dice (or use whole drumsticks)	2 red chili peppers, chopped	2 tsp white sugar
1 Tbsp minced garlic	¼ cup fermented salted black beans	1 Tbsp sesame oil
1 Tbsp chopped ginger	1 Tbsp dark soy sauce	

LIKE MOST family-style Filipino restaurants in Vancouver (or in the Philippines), North Vancouver's Fiesta is a designed like a cafeteria. Line up at the food counter, choose from the eight to ten items steaming away on hot plates that day and pay at the cash. More often than not, Chef Velasco is both tending the till and cooking up dishes in the back kitchen. She'll greet you just like a long-lost auntie. The place is often bustling with diners but also with Filipinos shopping at the food market that opens off the restaurant.

In the Philippines, this recipe is usually made with chicken feet, for economic reasons and for their distinct texture. There, they are a popular street food and commonly known as *adidas,* as in the running shoe! In Vancouver, however, this dish is more often made with chicken thighs or drumsticks instead because the meat is more tender. The fermented salted black beans called for in this recipe are available in cans, but substitute Chinese fermented dried black beans, which are sold in jars or plastic packages, if you can't find them. Serve this dish with steamed rice.

LINE A PLATE with paper towels. In a heavy frying pan, heat canola oil on high. Add chicken and brown on each side for 2 to 3 minutes. Using tongs, transfer chicken to the paper towel–lined plate to drain. Reserve the oil in the pan.

To the sizzling oil, add garlic, ginger, onions, chili peppers and black beans and sauté for 2 minutes. Stir in chicken, then add soy sauce, tomato paste and sugar, making sure to coat chicken evenly. Cook for 2 minutes, add 1 cup water and bring to a boil. Reduce the heat to medium, cover and cook for 10 minutes, or until liquid is reduced to a gravy. Drizzle sesame oil on top, then season with salt and freshly ground black pepper.

SIZZLING CHICKEN AND CLOUD EARS
in a Clay Pot
Serves 6

1 tsp sea salt

2 Tbsp light soy sauce

1 Tbsp Shaoxing rice wine

1 free-range chicken, 2 to 3 lbs, in bite-size pieces

1½ Tbsp vegetable oil

1 oz ginger, peeled and sliced

2 to 4 dried red chili peppers (halved, if you prefer more heat)

1 oz dried cloud ear fungus, rehydrated and cut in bite-size pieces

½ cup chicken stock

IN A LARGE bowl, combine sea salt, soy sauce and wine. Add chicken and, with a spoon, mix well until meat is well coated. Cover with plastic wrap, refrigerate and allow to marinate for at least 1 hour.

Heat vegetable oil in a wok on high, add ginger and chili peppers and allow to sizzle for 30 seconds. Stir in chicken and cook for 3 minutes. Pour in leftover marinade and cloud ears and sauté for another 3 minutes. Gently pour in chicken stock, cover and bring to a boil.

Transfer the contents of the wok to a large clay hot pot, cover and cook on medium-high heat for 5 minutes. Remove the lid and cook for another 5 minutes. Place the clay pot in the middle of the table and serve hot with steamed rice.

CHICKEN AND cloud ears are a favoured pair for hot pot–style recipes. A Chinese hot pot, not to be confused with the fondue-style meal also called hot pot, is traditionally a clay pot full of cooked food placed in the middle of the table. This dish, like many Chinese chicken recipes, calls for bone-in chicken because it's more succulent than the boneless cuts.

Cloud ear is one of the six major edible fungi (the others are guihua ear, silver ear, yue ear, yellow ear and stone ear), which are known to help reduce cholesterol, promote heart health and play an important role in vegetarian cuisine. Fresh cloud ears are hard to find, but dried ones make a good substitute. To rehydrate the cloud ears, rinse them first to remove any dirt or other impurities, then soak them in clean cold water for 20 to 30 minutes before cooking.

VICTORIA DRIVE

THE SIZABLE, FREE-STANDING 88 Supermarket on Victoria Drive at East 30th Avenue marks the beginning of a stretch of Chinese grocery stores, Asian bakeries, barbecue shops, makers and retailers of Chinese noodles and frozen dumplings, herbal shops, plus a wide selection of Asian restaurants, bubble tea cafés and Chinese fast-food outlets that run all the way to East 54th Avenue. It's a good glimpse into day-to-day life in some of the metropolitan cities in Asia.

With blocks of residents living in and around the neighbourhood, this area is where homemakers and seniors meet, eat in the nearby Chinese restaurants and Hong Kong–style cafés, and shop for groceries and barbecued goodies in the many Chinese supermarkets and meat shops along the way, any day of the week. On weekends and holidays, the foot and car traffic increases by at least a hundredfold as families and friends flock to restaurants like Western Lake Chinese Seafood Restaurant, Golden Swan Restaurant or Li Garden Seafood Restaurant for dim sum and dinner; to Kalvin's Szechuan Restaurant for potstickers and hot pots; to Mui Garden Restaurant for the Curry Beef Brisket and Hainanese Chicken. Teng's Market, the grocery store across from Western Lake, is a frequent stop for groceries to prepare a family feast. Down one block is Karmony Cake House, which sells gorgeous apple tarts, cocktail buns and wintermelon cakes.

VIETNAMESE GRILLED CHICKEN
with Lemon Grass
Serves 4

3 stalks lemon grass, chopped	1 tsp freshly ground black pepper	1 Tbsp vegetable oil
5 cloves garlic	1 Tbsp brown sugar	3 lbs skinless chicken thighs
5 shallots	2 Tbsp dark soy sauce	2 Tbsp canola oil
1 tsp salt	2 Tbsp hoisin sauce	

IN A FOOD processor, combine lemon grass, garlic, shallots, salt, black pepper, brown sugar, soy sauce, hoisin sauce and vegetable oil and purée for 3 to 4 minutes to make a paste. Transfer the mixture to a large bowl. (You can refrigerate this mixture in an airtight container for up to 3 days.) Add chicken and mix well to coat evenly with the sauce. Cover and refrigerate for at least 4 hours, or overnight if you desire.

In a large sauté pan with a lid, heat canola oil on medium-high, add chicken and brown for 5 minutes. Reduce the heat to medium, turn chicken over and brown for another 4 minutes. Add the lemon grass marinade, cover and cook for 3 minutes. Increase the heat to high and cook for 2 minutes. Season to taste with salt and serve hot.

USING FAMILY recipes passed down through the generations, Bon Café strives to offer authentic, honest Vietnamese cuisine. Among the popular dishes are Vietnamese spring rolls, salad rolls, grilled pork chops and bánh mì sandwiches. Grilled chicken is a classic Vietnamese meat dish served with plain rice or over noodle soup. This recipe, made with lemon grass, garlic, shallots and hoisin sauce as the predominant flavours, can be widely used to marinate chicken, ribs or lamb chops for the barbecue.

Lemon grass

RED CURRY DUCK

Serves 4

1 Tbsp dark soy sauce	5 garlic cloves, smashed	1 Tbsp canola oil
1 Tbsp light soy sauce	4 shallots, halved	4 bay leaves
1 whole duck, 3 to 3½ lbs, skin on	3 green onions, chopped	½ stick cane sugar
10 cups vegetable oil, for deep-frying	2 oz galangal, sliced	2 tomatoes, in wedges
1 Tbsp chopped Thai red chili pepper	1 tsp ground coriander	1 cup coconut milk
	2 Tbsp tomato paste	¼ cup chopped fresh cilantro
	3 Tbsp fish sauce	

START THIS recipe in the morning of the day before you plan to serve it, as it involves marinating the duck overnight plus another 3½ hours of hanging and deep-frying. You can skip this step by buying a Chinese barbecued duck instead and steaming it according to the recipe, but make sure you ask for the duck to be cut in half only rather than chopped into many pieces as is usual. This thick, creamy and beautifully coloured Thai curry has a subtle sweetness and a yogurty flavour that goes perfectly with the fattier, denser meat of the duck. Serve this dish with steamed jasmine rice or with the unleavened flatbread known as roti. You can find light-brown cane sugar sticks for this recipe in small boxes at Asian markets.

IN A SMALL bowl, combine dark and light soy sauces. Place duck in a non-reactive bowl. Using a pastry brush, evenly brush duck with soy sauces inside and out, cover and refrigerate overnight.

Cut a 2-foot piece of kitchen twine and place it on a clean work surface. Set the duck on top of it, drawing up the ends of the twine either side of the mid-section, then cross the twine as if you were tying a parcel, loop it around the wings and tie it securely so that the duck cannot fall out of its "harness." Form a loop at the end of the string and hang the duck, indoors, from a cabinet handle for at least 4 hours to dry out the meat. Set a dish below the duck to catch any drippings.

Line a large plate with paper towels. In a large 12-inch wok or a deep fryer, heat vegetable oil to 350°F. Add duck and cook for 10 to 15 minutes, then turn over and cook for another 10 to 15 minutes until skin is golden brown. Transfer duck to the paper towel–lined plate and allow to drain and dry for 30 minutes. Using a meat cleaver, cut duck in half lengthwise.

To steam the duck (whether marinated overnight or store bought), fill a large wok or a saucepan with a steamer insert with water and bring to a boil on high heat. Arrange duck halves in a bamboo steamer or in the steamer insert, cover and place in the wok or saucepan. Steam for 20 minutes, then remove from the heat and allow to cool to room temperature. Chop duck into large bite-size pieces.

In a food processor, combine chili peppers, garlic, shallots, green onions, galangal, coriander, tomato paste and fish sauce and blend until the mixture forms a paste.

In a wok, heat canola oil on high, then reduce the heat to low. Add curry paste, bay leaves and duck and stir to mix well. Increase the heat to medium and cook for 25 to 30 minutes. Stir in sugar stick, tomatoes and coconut milk and bring to a gentle boil. Reduce the heat to medium-low and simmer for 10 minutes. Garnish with chopped cilantro and serve.

ASIANS HAVE thousands of recipes for beef, goat, lamb and pork. No matter how the meats are cooked, they will be served cut up and, quite often, bone-in. If you wander the meat markets of Asia (or the meat section of Asian supermarkets in North America), you'll find oxtails, shanks, piles of briskets, tenderloins and flank steaks, which are the best cuts for pan-frying or stir-frying. And, of course, strips of honeycomb-patterned tripe, plump red hearts and smooth, tender livers.

In Asia, goat is as popular as lamb. Both are used in India, where Hindus consider the cow sacred and so don't eat beef. Goat is usually braised, as in the Nepalese Goat Curry, until the meat falls off the bone and melts in your mouth. In North America, look for fresh or frozen goat meat in Indian, Chinese and halal meat shops. Lamb is often served as a chop in India but rarely elsewhere. Try the Pondicherry Minted Lamb Chops, or visit the Richmond or Chinatown night markets to taste lamb skewers grilled over open fires and served smoking hot.

Except for Muslims, who avoid pork, Asians don't leave any part of the pig to waste. From the head to the trotters, eating the whole animal is a sign of the highest respect for the life it sacrificed to become food for humans. Try the traditional Chinese Roasted Crispy-Skin Pork, which is rubbed with five-spice powder and galangal and slow cooked for hours, or try the Humba-Style Braised Pork Belly, a festive Filipino dish simmered with ginger and garlic, chilies and star anise and served with banana flowers.

MEATS

BEEF CROQUETTES
(Bagadel Cabe)
Serves 6 to 8

1 medium Russet potato, peeled and diced

½ lb ground beef

1 egg, separated

1 tsp freshly ground white pepper

2 Tbsp cornstarch

½ tsp salt or to taste

¼ tsp ground nutmeg

1 medium onion, finely chopped

1 Tbsp bread crumbs

3 Tbsp vegetable oil

SPICE ISLANDS Indonesian Restaurant is tucked away in Kerrisdale, in an area with very few eateries. However, the restaurant has a loyal following and consistently wins awards for its traditional Indonesian food made with locally sourced products. It's also one of the few Asian restaurants in the city with a notable wine list.

This classic Indonesian side dish can also be eaten as a snack. Arrange the croquettes on a large platter, family-style, and serve them with a variety of appetizers and more substantial dishes, mounds of rice and an array of sambals and condiments.

PLACE POTATOES IN a microwave-safe container, add ¼ cup water, cover and cook on high for 5 minutes. Drain off and discard any remaining liquid, then mash potatoes. Add ground beef and, using a fork, mix until well combined. Stir in egg yolk until well mixed. Add white pepper, cornstarch, salt, nutmeg and onions and mix thoroughly. Using your hands, scoop a small handful of the meat mixture into your palm. Roll it into a patty about 4 to 5 inches around and ¼ inch thick. Place patty on a large plate. Repeat with the remaining beef mixture. You should have 6 to 8 patties.

Place egg white in a small bowl and beat with a fork until foamy. Arrange bread crumbs on a large shallow plate. Dip patties first in the egg white, then in bread crumbs, tapping them lightly to remove any excess.

Line a large plate with paper towels. Heat vegetable oil in a frying pan on medium-high. Add patties, 2 or 3 at a time, and pan-fry on one side for 2 minutes. Turn patty over and cook for 2 minutes more, or until golden brown. Allow to drain on the paper towel–lined plate. Serve hot.

CUBED BEEF TENDERLOIN
with Basil
Serves 2

6 oz beef tenderloin, in 1-inch dice	1 cup vegetable oil, for deep-frying	4 Tbsp chopped basil
2 tsp light soy sauce	1 small onion, sliced	1 Tbsp fish sauce
1 tsp cornstarch	1 clove garlic, finely chopped	1 Tbsp Maggi sauce
1 egg white	½ tsp coarsely ground black pepper	2 tsp white sugar
½ cup all-purpose flour		

IN A LARGE bowl, toss beef with soy sauce, cornstarch and egg white until well coated. Set aside.

Line a plate with paper towels. Place flour in a shallow dish. In a wok, bring vegetable oil to a boil on high heat. Using a slotted spoon, roll beef cubes in flour, shaking off any excess. Carefully place beef cubes in oil and blanch for 90 seconds. Using a slotted spoon, transfer beef to the paper towel–lined plate to drain. Set aside. (Allow the oil to cool to room temperature, then pour into a glass jar and reserve for another use.)

In another wok or a frying pan, heat 1 tsp of the vegetable oil used to fry the beef on high. Add onions, garlic and black pepper and brown for 45 seconds. Stir in basil, fish sauce, Maggi sauce and sugar and mix well. Stir in beef and sauté for 2 minutes until warmed through. Serve hot.

KIRIN IS one of the few Chinese restaurant groups known for fine dining not only in British Columbia but throughout North America. Each of the five restaurants in the group—all of them in or near Vancouver—has a different character, but all maintain the same award-winning standards of food and service.

Incorporating fresh herbs such as basil is not common in traditional Chinese cooking. This recipe, which features freshly chopped and sautéed basil, is considered a New World Chinese dish. Serve it with bowls of steamed rice.

LARB BEEF

Serves 2

5 long red or green chili peppers	½ cup chicken stock	1 green onion, chopped
3 whole green cardamom pods	3 Tbsp fish sauce	3 shallots, thinly sliced
4 black peppercorns	⅓ cup minced hanger steak	1 bunch fresh cilantro, rinsed and stems removed
4 white peppercorns	2 Tbsp fresh kaffir lime juice	¼ cup pork crackling, in pieces
2 blades mace	½ tsp white sugar	4 whole dried chili peppers, for garnish (optional)
1 whole star anise	1 tsp ground lemon grass	
2 Tbsp ground galangal	4 Vietnamese mint leaves, coarsely chopped	
¼ cup uncooked jasmine rice		

MAENAM is known for beautifully plated, authentic Thai food with a contemporary twist that perfectly balances the hot, sweet, salty and sour flavours of this cuisine. Before opening his own restaurant, Chef An worked with such culinary masters as Jacques Pépin and David Thompson, and it shows. Among the many award-winning dishes, the Royal Thai Dinner, a grand tasting menu for Asian food lovers, is not to be missed. Maenam also offers a sophisticated wine list that's one of the best among Vancouver's Asian restaurants.

Fresh herbs and spices are the key to this warm Laotian salad made with minced meat and ground roasted rice. Seasoned with lime and fish sauce, it's a refreshing summer appetizer or a light meal. Pork crackling, deep-fried and sun-dried pig skin, is sold in bags at Chinese meat shops.

PREHEAT A TOASTER oven to 300°F. In a small bowl, combine chili peppers, cardamom, black and white peppercorns, mace and star anise until well mixed. Arrange on the toaster oven tray and roast for 5 to 7 minutes, or until chili peppers begin to brown. Transfer the spices to a mortar and grind with a pestle for about 10 minutes, or until spices become a powder. Add ground galangal, mix well and transfer to a small airtight container. This is your spice mix and will keep refrigerated for up to 10 days. Clean, rinse and dry the mortar and pestle for later use.

Heat a frying pan on high. Add rice, reduce the heat to medium and roast, stirring constantly to prevent burning, for 5 to 7 minutes until golden. Turn off the heat. Transfer rice to the mortar and grind for 3 to 5 minutes until sandy. Set aside.

In a medium saucepan, combine chicken stock, 2 Tbsp of the fish sauce, minced steak and 1 tsp of the spice mix. Cook on medium heat for 3 to 5 minutes, stirring occasionally, until beef is well cooked and has absorbed some of the liquid. Using a slotted spoon, transfer beef to a large bowl, draining off any excess liquid. (Discard the remaining cooking liquid, or reserve it to enjoy as a dipping sauce for breads and buns.) To the beef, add the remaining 1 Tbsp fish sauce, lime juice, sugar and lemon grass and toss well. Stir in rice powder, mint, green onions and shallots and toss gently. Garnish with cilantro and pork crackling and whole chili peppers. Scoop the salad into a large serving bowl and serve family-style.

BRAISED FIVE-SPICE BEEF SHANK

Serves 4 to 6

SPICE SACHET

¼ cup whole star anise	⅛ cup whole cloves
2 cinnamon sticks, crushed	⅛ cup Szechuan peppercorns
	4 Tbsp fennel seeds

LONG'S NOODLE House surprises a lot of first-timers who find it hard to believe that such high-quality authentic Shanghai home-style cooking can come out of such a tiny place. It's owned and operated by a Shanghainese couple: Chef Sun takes care of all the food shopping, preparation and cooking, while his wife, Sandy, attends to diners in the thirty-five-seat restaurant. Once a hidden gem, Long's is now regarded as one of the top ten Shanghai restaurants in Metro Vancouver and regularly has lineups. It's worth the wait.

The robust spice mix used to make this braising stock is also used to flavour nearly all Chinese five-spice recipes for meats, eggs, chicken wings and even vegetarian dishes. The marinade made with the mix is used repeatedly as a braising stock, as a reduction, as a seasoning agent or simply as a condiment.

Like many braised dishes, this is a recipe that keeps well and tastes even better the next day. If time allows, leave the shanks in the pot and cover it overnight. Before serving, gently reheat the beef on medium heat, then transfer the shank to a serving platter, allow to cool for 5 minutes and slice. Serve this beef shank with steamed buns or as a topping for noodle soups. Refrigerate the leftover braising stock in an airtight container for up to 3 months—just be sure to bring it to a boil once a week to ward off any bacterial growth.

SPICE SACHET Make a spice sachet by placing a 6-inch square piece of cheesecloth on a clean work surface. Arrange the star anise, cinnamon, cloves, peppercorns and fennel in the middle of the cheesecloth. Gather the corners of the cheesecloth, completely encasing the spices, and tie tightly with a piece of kitchen twine. (You can also use a store-bought fish bag or herb bag, available in Asian markets, instead of a cheesecloth to hold the spices.)

BRAISED BEEF SHANK To a medium saucepan on medium heat, add sea salt, peppercorns and white sugar. Immediately reduce the heat to low, stir and cook the spices for 90 seconds, then turn off the heat. Remove the pan from the heat and allow the mixture to cool to room temperature, 15 to 20 minutes.

Add beef to the spice mixture and roll it around until evenly coated. Cover beef with plastic wrap and refrigerate for at least 2 hours.

Rinse off the beef. In a medium pot, combine beef, spice sachet, 6 cups water, ginger, dark and light soy sauces and brown sugar. Bring to a boil on high heat, then reduce the heat to medium, cover and cook for 30 minutes. Reduce the heat to a simmer and cook, covered, for 2 to 3 hours, or until meat is fork-tender.

BRAISED BEEF SHANK

3 tsp sea salt

3 tsp Szechuan peppercorns

1 Tbsp white sugar

2 lbs beef shank, rinsed and patted dry

6 oz ginger, unpeeled and cut in ¼-inch slices

1 cup dark soy sauce

1 cup light soy sauce

¼ cup brown sugar (or ½ stick cane sugar)

4 Tbsp chopped fresh cilantro

Transfer the beef to a carving board, reserving the braising liquid, and allow it to rest for 10 to 15 minutes. Slice beef into ⅛-inch slices. Transfer to a serving platter, drizzle with 2 Tbsp braising liquid and garnish with pinches of cilantro.

(Allow the remaining braising liquid to cool to room temperature, then transfer to an airtight container and refrigerate for another use.)

NEPALESE GOAT CURRY

Serves 4 to 6

4 Tbsp canola oil	2 medium tomatoes, chopped	10 oz boneless goat meat, fat removed, in 1-inch cubes
¼ tsp mustard seeds	¼ tsp turmeric	
¼ tsp cumin seeds	¼ tsp coriander	¼ tsp garam masala
2 medium onions, sliced	¼ tsp curry powder	1 tsp salt
3 cloves garlic, minced	¼ tsp freshly ground black pepper	1 tsp fresh lime juice
2 Tbsp minced ginger	1 bay leaf	½ cup fresh cilantro leaves

HEAT CANOLA OIL in a heavy-bottomed saucepan on medium-high, then add mustard and cumin seeds and brown for 30 seconds. Stir in onions, garlic and ginger and cook until golden brown, 8 to 10 minutes.

Increase the heat to high, pour in tomatoes and cook for 5 minutes, stirring frequently, until the liquid reduces. Stir in turmeric, coriander, curry powder, black pepper and bay leaf, then add goat meat and stir gently until evenly coated. Slowly add ½ cup water, mix well, cover and bring to a boil. Reduce the heat to a simmer, cover and cook for 20 to 30 minutes or until a thin layer of oil coats the surface.

Stir in garam masala, add ¼ cup water, mix well, cover and cook for 10 minutes. Add another ¼ cup water, stirring it into the meat, then cover and cook for 10 minutes. Add a final ¼ cup water, cover and cook until meat is fork-tender and the sauce is thick and almost forms a paste. Season with salt and lime juice, cover and simmer for 3 minutes. Turn off the heat and allow it to rest for an hour or overnight to allow the flavours to meld. When ready to serve, gently reheat the curry on medium heat, transfer to a large serving bowl and garnish with cilantro. Serve hot.

NEPALESE CUISINE combines elements of Indian, Chinese and Tibetan cooking along with an assortment of herbs and spices. The secret to success for this recipe is to add small amounts of water a few times during the simmering process. Let the water work as a reducing agent to blend and seal in all the flavours and fragrances.

Like most curries, stews and braised meat recipes, this dish will taste even better the next day. Refrigerate leftovers in an airtight container for up to 3 days, or freeze the goat curry for up to 2 weeks. Serve this curry with steamed rice or roti.

LEMON GRASS LAMB CHOPS

Serves 4

LEMON GRASS MARINADE

3 stalks fresh lemon grass

1 red hot chili pepper, chopped

½ tsp chopped garlic

1 tsp freshly cracked black pepper

½ tsp salt

3 tsp palm sugar

3 Tbsp fish sauce

1 tsp fresh lemon juice

1 Tbsp sweet mushroom soy sauce (or dark soy sauce)

MOST HOTELS in Vancouver now offer at least a few Asian dishes or infuse their recipes with Asian flavours. The menu at the Coast Hotel is no different; however, this Vietnamese recipe comes from Chef Thai's own family collection.

When finely chopped to deliver its potent flavour to the fullest, and with the help of fish sauce and sweet mushroom sauce, lemon grass neutralizes the gamey taste of lamb chops. This delicious marinade also complements other meat chops, such as pork chops and chicken thighs. This recipe calls for searing, then baking, the chops, but feel free to pan-fry or barbecue them, if you prefer. Serve the chops with steamed rice.

LEMON GRASS MARINADE Using a sharp knife, cut each lemon grass stalk 3 to 4 inches from the bottom, where the light and green portions meet. Peel and discard the top layer of the light part of each stalks, revealing the tender, white inner hearts. Slice these and mince them finely. (Reserve the remaining green leaves to use in other dishes.) In a medium bowl, combine lemon grass, chili peppers, garlic, black pepper, salt, sugar, fish sauce, lemon juice and soy sauce and stir until well mixed.

MARINATED LAMB CHOPS Place lemon grass marinade in a large shallow pan. Add lamb chops individually, spooning marinade all over the meat to ensure each chop is well coated. Cover with plastic wrap and refrigerate for 3 hours or up to 24 hours.

To make nuoc mam dipping sauce, in a saucepan combine 1 cup water, garlic and brown sugar and bring to a boil on medium-high heat. Reduce the heat to medium-low, stirring constantly for 1 minute until sugar melts, then turn off the heat. Add lemon juice, vinegar and chili peppers, stir well and transfer to a sauce bowl. (Will keep refrigerated in an airtight container for 3 to 4 weeks.)

MARINATED LAMB CHOPS

4 large lamb chops, each 8 oz
(or 8 small chops, each 4 oz)

2 cloves garlic, crushed

2 Tbsp brown sugar

2 Tbsp fresh lemon juice

2 Tbsp white wine vinegar

1 Thai bird's eye
chili pepper, chopped

1 Tbsp canola oil

½ cucumber, diced

1 small tomato, diced

2 Tbsp chopped
fresh cilantro

About 30 minutes before cooking, remove lamb chops from the refrigerator. Preheat the oven to 400°F. In an ovenproof pan, heat canola oil on high. Add lamb chops, reserving the marinade, and brown on one side for 2 minutes. Turn lamb over and brown for another 2 minutes, then transfer to the oven and bake for 5 to 10 minutes, or until cooked to your liking. Remove from the oven and transfer to a serving plate. Set aside.

Transfer the marinade to a small saucepan and bring to a gentle boil on medium-high. Reduce the heat to low, simmer for 5 minutes and then pour into a serving bowl.

Place cucumbers, tomatoes and cilantro in individual serving bowls. Serve lamb chops, family-style, with the marinade, nuoc mam dipping sauce, cucumbers, tomatoes and cilantro as condiments.

PONDICHERRY MINTED LAMB CHOPS

Serves 4

FRIED ONIONS

1 Tbsp ghee (or canola oil)

1 small yellow onion, in ⅛-inch slices

½ tsp chopped ginger

½ tsp chopped red chili pepper

½ tsp chopped garlic

MINTED LAMB CHOPS

1 oz fried onions

2 Tbsp canola oil

1½ tsp finely minced garlic

1½ tsp finely minced ginger

5 Tbsp tomato paste

¼ tsp turmeric

⅛ tsp cayenne pepper

½ tsp ground cumin

½ tsp ground coriander

3½ Tbsp tamarind sauce

8 lamb chops, each 4 to 6 oz

7 Tbsp whipping cream

1 tsp ground mint

1 bunch fresh mint

PUDUCHERRY (FORMERLY known as Pondicherry) is a Union Territory located in the southeastern part of India. It was once a French colony, and French flavours and heritage, lifestyle and culinary influence still linger strongly in this region. Drawing on the traditional European lamb and mint combination, this dish adds crimini mushrooms, whipping cream and distinctly Indian spices.

Serve this dish family-style, or take it to work or school in a stainless steel tiffin container. Curry 2 U is an Indian fast-food restaurant on Granville Island, which sees thousands of locals and tourists every year. To reduce waste, Chef Jamal has been serving food in traditional reusable thalis and tiered tiffins, which saves 100,000 paper plates and Styrofoam containers annually.

FRIED ONIONS Heat ghee (or canola oil) in a frying pan on medium-high, then add onions and brown for 2 minutes. Stir in ginger, chili peppers and garlic and sauté for another minute. Reduce the heat to medium, allow to cook for 90 seconds then remove from the heat and set aside. Will keep refrigerated in an airtight container for up to 3 days.

MINTED LAMB CHOPS In a blender, purée onions, 1 Tbsp of the canola oil, garlic, ginger, tomato paste, turmeric, cayenne, cumin, coriander, tamarind sauce and ⅝ cup water to a smooth paste.

In a large nonstick frying pan, heat the remaining 1 Tbsp canola oil on high. Add lamb chops and brown on one side for 2 minutes. Turn chops over and brown for another 2 minutes. Using tongs, transfer chops to a plate and drain and discard any liquid from the frying pan.

Return the frying pan to medium-high heat. Stir in the spicy paste mixture. Add lamb chops, coat them evenly with the paste and cook for 15 to 20 minutes, or until lamb is cooked to your liking. Reduce the heat to low, add whipping cream and ground mint and simmer for 3 minutes. Season with salt to taste. Arrange chops on a large serving platter, garnish with fresh mint and serve.

LAMB JALFREZI

Serves 4 to 6

6 oz cauliflower, roughly chopped

2 medium Russet potatoes, skin on, roughly chopped

1 large carrot, roughly chopped

3 Tbsp vegetable oil

1 lb lamb tenderloin, in 1-inch dice

1 Tbsp cumin seeds

2 bay leaves

1 large onion, chopped

1 Tbsp finely chopped garlic

1 Tbsp finely chopped ginger

1 Tbsp tomato paste

1 tsp white sugar

2 to 4 green chili peppers (optional)

1 tsp turmeric

2 medium tomatoes, chopped

4 oz crimini mushrooms, quartered

½ cup green peas (fresh or frozen)

2 Tbsp chopped fresh cilantro

PLACE CAULIFLOWER, POTATOES and carrots in a microwave-safe container, cover and cook for 5 minutes on high. Drain and discard any liquid from the container and set aside.

In a large saucepan, heat 2 Tbsp of the vegetable oil on medium-high. Add lamb and cook for 3 minutes. Using a slotted spoon, transfer meat to a large plate.

Add the remaining 1 Tbsp vegetable oil to the pan, then stir in cumin seeds and bay leaves. When the spices start to sizzle, 20 to 30 seconds, add onions and cook for 3 to 4 minutes or until golden brown. Add garlic, ginger and tomato paste, stir and cook for 2 minutes. Stir in sugar, chili peppers and turmeric and cook for another minute. Return lamb to the pan, add tomatoes and ¼ cup water, stir and cook for 1 minute. Reduce the heat to medium-low, cover and simmer for 5 minutes.

Add mushrooms and peas and mix well. Stir in the reserved vegetables and cook for 2 minutes. Transfer the curry to a large serving bowl, garnish with cilantro and serve immediately.

JALFREZI MAY be an example of the influence Chinese cooking has had on Indian cuisine in the big cities of India. This style of dish combines meats stir-fried in oil with curry and other spices. A healthy recipe, jalfrezi can be mild like many stir fries (without the chilies) or fiery hot like many curries (with the chilies added). Take away the meat, and jalfrezi becomes a vegetarian delight. Serve this dish with Indian breads, such as naan or chapatti, or with basmati rice.

INDONESIAN SPICY PORK

Serves 4

2 Tbsp extra-virgin olive oil	2 cloves garlic, finely chopped	1 tsp salt
1 lb lean boneless pork, sliced or diced	1 tsp finely chopped ginger	1 tsp white sugar
	1 tsp sambal oelek	2 green onions, chopped
1 medium onion, finely chopped	1 tsp kecap manis	

THIS INTENSELY flavoured dish shows off Indonesia's number one chili sauce—the hot and spicy sambal oelek, made from chilies, sugar and salt—which can be used in cooking or as a condiment. Kecap manis is a sweet Indonesian soy sauce that's thicker and more intensely flavoured than Chinese soy sauces. A little goes a long way. Look for sambal oelek and kecap manis in Asian supermarkets. Serve this dish with lots of steamed rice.

IN A DEEP sauté pan, heat 1 Tbsp of the olive oil on medium-high. Add pork and brown for 3 minutes. Add the remaining 1 Tbsp olive oil, stir in onions and garlic and sauté for 2 to 3 minutes, or until onions are golden brown. Add ginger, sambal oelek, kecap manis, salt and sugar, stir well and sauté for 30 seconds. Reduce the heat to medium, add ¼ cup water, then cover and cook for 20 minutes. Reduce the heat to low, add green onions and sauté for 2 minutes. Transfer to a serving platter and serve hot.

To GRASP HOW significant Vancouver's Korean communities are, look no farther than North Road and Lougheed Highway, where two of the largest Korean supermarkets, Han Nam and H-Mart, stand facing each other. Although both are on North Road, where the first wave of Korean immigrants settled in the early 1990s, municipal zoning puts Han Nam in Burnaby and H-Mart in Coquitlam, otherwise known by many as Koreatown. At these supermarkets, allow yourself time to browse the vegetable section for unfamiliar produce such as fresh Korean ginseng and the aisles of ready-to-eat pickles, cooked food, meats, seafood, Japanese ingredients and fresh Korean pastries. Soak up the smells of garlic and seafood, as you wander the aisles with local workers stopping in for lunch and home cooks and older couples doing their grocery shopping.

Although North Road still has an abundance of Korean shops and eateries, such as Insadong, which is always packed and offers a huge variety of Korean barbecue dishes and set dinners, and Wang Ga Ma Korean Restaurant, which is much smaller but serves homestyle beef dishes, many Korean restaurants have spread to Surrey and Langley. Local Koreans consider Buk Jang Do Ga on Fraser Highway their kitchen away from home when looking for comforting dishes such as mung bean cake. The recent opening of another H-Mart on the same road signals just how many Koreans are now living in the suburbs.

Although barbecue (gogi gui, bulgogi and other meats grilled over gas or charcoal) is still the most-ordered item in most Korean restaurants, other authentic and addictive dishes include soft and silky tofu soup (soon doo boo jigae), kimbap (Korean rice rolls served with kimchi), savoury pancakes and clear but very fragrant beef soups.

NORTH ROAD

PORK IN A SPICY TARO-COCONUT SAUCE
(Pork Laing) with Smoked Scads
Serves 4

10 oz fresh taro leaves
(or 4 oz dried leaves)

2 Tbsp vegetable oil

4 cloves garlic, minced

1 Tbsp finely chopped ginger

1 small onion, chopped

1 lb pork tenderloin, in 1-inch dice

2 smoked round scads, in 2-inch lengths

1 small tomato, chopped

1 Tbsp shrimp paste

1 Tbsp chili paste

1 can (450 mL) coconut milk

1 medium Japanese eggplant, in 1-inch-thick logs

1 cup peeled and diced kabocha squash

LAING IS a popular Filipino dish of the Bicol Region, in which taro leaves, known as *gabi*, are the main vegetable cooked in a spicy and creamy coconut sauce. Fresh taro leaves are hard to find, so substitute packaged sun-dried ones, which are available year-round in Filipino markets. (Note that fresh taro leaves should not be eaten raw, as they are toxic, and must be thoroughly cooked.) If you really can't find taro leaves, try kale instead. Round scads are 4 to 6 inches long, and packages of the wood-smoked fish can be found in the freezer section of Filipino markets. Serve this traditional favourite with steamed rice.

FILL A LARGE bowl with water, add taro leaves and soak for 10 minutes (fresh leaves) to 30 minutes (dried leaves). Rinse fresh leaves under cold running water and place in a colander to drain (or gently squeeze dried leaves in your hands to remove any excess moisture). Set aside.

In a large frying pan, heat vegetable oil on high, then add garlic, ginger and onions and sauté for 2 minutes. Add pork and round scads and sauté for another 2 minutes. Stir in tomatoes, taro leaves, shrimp paste and chili paste, mix well and cook for 2 to 3 minutes. Pour in coconut milk and ½ cup water, stirring gently, and bring to a boil. Add eggplant and squash and sauté for 3 minutes, then reduce the heat to medium-low, cover and braise for 10 minutes. Transfer to a large family-style platter and serve hot.

WUXI RIBS WITH BLANCHED SPINACH

Serves 4 to 6

1-inch piece of fresh ginger, skin on, in 6 thick slices

2 green onions in 2-inch lengths

2 lbs pork side ribs, in 3- to 4-inch lengths

3 Tbsp + ½ tsp canola oil

1 cinnamon stick

1 brown sugar stick (or ½ cup brown sugar)

1 tsp five-spice powder

10 whole star anise

1 tsp Szechuan peppercorns

1 cup chicken stock

¼ cup dark soy sauce

¼ cup Shaoxing rice wine

1 bunch spinach, stems removed, washed, drained and leaves roughly cut in half

IN A WOK, bring 4 cups water to a boil on high heat. Add 4 of the ginger slices and green onions. Blanch ribs for 5 minutes, then, using tongs, transfer to a colander to drain. Discard the ginger, green onions and blanching liquid.

Preheat the oven to 400°F. Using a pastry brush, lightly and evenly coat ribs with 3 Tbsp canola oil. Arrange them on a baking sheet and bake for 15 minutes. Remove the baking sheet from the oven and, using tongs, turn ribs over. Bake for another 10 minutes. Remove from the oven and set aside. (This step seals in the moisture in the ribs.)

In a medium saucepan, bring the remaining 2 slices of ginger, cinnamon stick, sugar stick, five-spice powder, star anise, peppercorns, chicken stock, soy sauce and wine to a boil on high heat. Add ribs, season with salt and cook for 10 minutes. Reduce the heat to medium-low, cover and simmer for 20 to 25 minutes, or until ribs are fork-tender.

Just before serving, bring a medium pot of water to a boil on high heat. Add spinach and ½ tsp canola oil and blanch for 90 seconds. Drain spinach in a colander, pressing out any excess water with a spatula, and transfer to a deep serving dish. Arrange ribs over the spinach. Drizzle 3 to 4 Tbsp rib cooking liquid over the meat and serve the remaining liquid in a sauce bowl in case guests want extra sauce. Serve hot with steamed buns or rice.

WUXI, a bustling city in Jiangsu Province known for its silk, is located 2 hours outside Shanghai and is often referred to as Little Shanghai for its exceptional cuisine. Spareribs cooked Wuxi-style incorporate five-spice marinade, ginger and wine. One of the province's signature dishes, this popular pork recipe is also served in many Mandarin restaurants around the country.

CHINESE BBQ PORK

(Char Siu)

Serves 6 to 8

3 Tbsp dark soy sauce	6 whole green onions, smashed	¼ cup tomato paste
1 Tbsp sambal oelek	6 cloves garlic, smashed	1 tsp white sugar
1 Tbsp sesame oil	½ bunch fresh cilantro	3 to 4 lbs skinless,
¼ cup peeled and sliced ginger	¼ cup Shaoxing rice wine	boneless pork shoulder

WILD RICE was the first modern Chinese restaurant to combine traditional recipes with modern cooking techniques and bistro-style plating. The open-concept room has high ceilings and a handsome bar that offers the best wine-pairing menu among Vancouver's Chinese restaurants. Fittingly, owner Andrew Wong's grandfather once owned the Lotus Hotel just down the street from this award-winning Pender Street restaurant.

In Chinese, *char siu* literally means "barbecue on a skewer" and is a favoured Cantonese-style roasted pork. Traditionally, skewers of pork were barbecued by hand over open charcoal stoves. Nowadays, they are hung and roasted in vertical ovens. For smaller quantities, such as this recipe, your home oven will suffice. You will need to marinate the meat for 12 to 24 hours, but the actual roasting time is only about an hour. Wrapped in foil and placed in an airtight container, it can be frozen for up to 10 days. Leftover char siu can be diced and added to fried rice, or sliced and added to chow mein.

IN A LARGE, nonreactive bowl, combine soy sauce, sambal oelek, sesame oil, ginger, green onions, garlic, cilantro, wine, tomato paste and sugar and allow the flavours to meld for at least 1 hour.

Trim and discard excess fat from pork, then cut meat in 1-inch-thick strips. Place pork in the marinade, mix until well coated and cover tightly with plastic wrap (or transfer to an airtight container) and refrigerate for at least 12 hours, if not for a full 24 hours.

To cook pork, remove the top rack from the oven. Half-fill a large baking pan with water and place it on the bottom rack, making sure there is enough room to put the top rack back in the oven. Preheat the oven to 475°F. Remove pork from the refrigerator.

Arrange pork strips in the middle of the top rack, at least 1 inch apart. Slide the rack back into the oven, positioning it so that the strips are over the baking pan. Bake for 20 minutes.

Reduce the temperature to 325°F and bake for 17 minutes, brushing both sides of pork strips with marinade every few minutes.

Reduce the temperature to 200°F and bake for another 10 minutes. Remove the top rack from the oven and allow pork to cool for 8 minutes. Cut into ½-inch-thick slices and serve on a large platter.

OVEN-ROASTED PORK TORO

Serves 3 to 4

1 tsp curry powder	1 tsp light soy sauce
½ tsp paprika	1 tsp white sugar
1 stalk lemon grass, chopped	3 strips pork toro, each 6 oz
1 tsp dark soy sauce	

IN A MEDIUM bowl, combine curry powder, paprika, lemon grass, dark and light soy sauces and sugar. Whisk until well mixed. Add pork and toss gently until the meat is evenly coated. Cover and refrigerate overnight or for at least 10 hours.

Preheat the oven to 350°F. In a grill pan fitted with a lightly greased wire rack, cook pork for 20 minutes. Increase the oven temperature to 400°F, carefully turn pork over and bake for 15 minutes. Remove pork from the oven and allow to cool for 5 to 10 minutes. Cut in ¼-inch-thick slices, transfer to a large serving platter and serve family-style.

WHEN TROPIKA first opened on Cambie Street in 1990, it was the first Asian restaurant to offer Malaysian, Singaporean and Thai food under one roof. There are now three restaurants, including one on Robson Street downtown and another at Aberdeen Centre in Richmond, offering not only the traditional satays, curries and gorengs but also exquisitely prepared specialty courses such as lobster tom yum kung and Thai-style yum chicken feet.

Pork toro is the layer of light-coloured meat found right below the spine that partly covers the rib cage. The meat is well marbled, very tender and only about a quarter-inch thick, and it becomes both crunchy and chewy when cooked. Be careful not to overcook it. This Malaysian-spiced version combines sweet, salty and hot flavours that taste even better when left to infuse overnight, so begin making this appetizer-style dish the day before you plan to serve it.

KINGSWAY, METRO VANCOUVER'S longest street, starts at Main Street near Broadway in Vancouver and runs southeast all the way to the Burnaby/New Westminster border. Most of the retail outlets along this street are Asian restaurants and stores: from Indian dosa, Vietnamese pho' and Korean barbecue restaurants to Taiwanese bubble tea cafés, Mandarin noodle houses and even Filipino restaurants! The grocery stores and markets are mostly Chinese, Vietnamese and Korean.

Most of the restaurants occur in clusters. Within a few blocks between Fraser and Knight, for example, are Po Kong Vegetarian Restaurant, an eatery devoted to meat-free ingredients; Tung Hing Bakery, which is famous for its bánh mì sandwiches; and the equally well-known House of Dosas. Two Cantonese places—Ken's Chinese Restaurant (for golden B.C. Dungeness crab) and Dai Tung (for five-cup spiced duck)—face each other on the same block.

East of Willingdon Avenue, near Metrotown, are modern Taiwanese café restaurants: Tea Works (the original is still on Victoria Drive), The One Restaurant and 508 Bistro are popular late-night joints. Hanwoori Korean Restaurant's, famous barbecue and authentic homestyle fare is just blocks away.

For a hot-and-spicy challenge, go to Hotluck and order the red-hot Szechuan hot pot or to Curry King Café, which offers an extensive menu of curries and multi-course dinners. Farther down, near Imperial Street, is the unlikely Greek-turned-Vietnamese restaurant, Pho' Hong, known for its soup, and on nearby side streets are two Hunan restaurants, one of which is the award-winning Alvin Garden. Be sure to try its marinated pork heart.

During the day, you're likely to share these restaurants with large parties of girlfriends, homemakers and youngsters, or with moms and schoolkids having lunch. In the evening, many places—particularly the smaller family-style ones—are filled with locals from the newly built high-rise condos and townhouses all along this corridor.

BURMESE-STYLE PORK CURRY
Serves 4

BURMESE CURRY PASTE

5 dried green or red chili peppers, seeded, soaked for 15 minutes and drained

2 stalks lemon grass, coarsely chopped

2 oz galangal, coarsely chopped

4 oz ginger, in ⅛-inch slices

4 Tbsp turmeric

4 shallots, sliced

¼ cup chopped garlic

1 Tbsp coriander seeds

1 tsp ground cumin

4 to 5 whole star anise

⅓ piece cassia bark (pounded in a mortar to break into small pieces)

3 whole cloves

2 whole pods Thai cardamom

BURMESE PORK

4 lbs pork shoulder, deboned and cut in 1-inch cubes

2 Tbsp vegetable oil

½ cup minced ginger

¼ cup chopped garlic

¼ cup Burmese curry paste

2 oz roasted whole peanuts

4 shallots, quartered

6 cloves pickled garlic

2 cups chicken stock

1 Tbsp palm sugar

1 Tbsp tamarind sauce

1 Tbsp fish sauce

BURMESE CURRY PASTE In a food processor, combine chili peppers, lemon grass, galangal, ginger, turmeric, shallots, garlic, coriander, cumin, star anise, cassia bark, cloves and Thai cardamom and purée for 30 seconds on low. Increase the speed to high and purée for 2 to 3 minutes until ingredients form a paste.

BURMESE PORK In a medium saucepan, bring pork and 5 cups cold water to a boil on high heat and cook for 2 minutes. Drain in a colander, rinse under cold running water and pat dry.

In a large sauté pan, heat vegetable oil on high, add ginger and chopped garlic and sauté until golden, about 1 minute. Stir in Burmese curry paste, then add pork, peanuts, shallots, pickled garlic and chicken stock. Reduce the heat to low and simmer for 30 to 40 minutes until pork is fork-tender. Season with sugar, tamarind sauce and fish sauce and cook for another 2 to 3 minutes. Transfer to a large serving bowl and serve immediately.

INFLUENCED BY Chinese, Southeast Asian and Indian cuisines, Burmese food ranges from mild to fiery spicy, cold to hot, and includes salads, noodle soups loaded with interesting toppings, roti and samosas.

The robust curry paste used in this dish is so fragrant and gratifying that you many want to double the recipe. Refrigerate any leftovers in an airtight container for up to 2 weeks. And although you can buy pickled garlic in jars or cans at Asian markets, try making your own. Bring 1 cup each of white rice vinegar and cold water, 2 Tbsp salt, 2 Tbsp white sugar and 20 to 24 cloves of peeled garlic to a full boil, then transfer the contents to a sterilized 2½-cup jar and refrigerate for 2 days. They can be stored in the brine for up to 3 months.

Thai cardamoms, called *kra-waan* in Thai, are creamy in colour and available in specialty food stores. You can substitute green cardamoms if you can't find them.

Serve this curry with bowls of steamed Thai jasmine rice.

HUMBA-STYLE BRAISED PORK BELLY

Serves 8 to 10

6 whole star anise	20 cloves garlic, peeled	1 cup cane or coconut vinegar
5 dried red chili peppers	1 cup diced ginger	¼ cup brown sugar
⅛ cup black peppercorns	2 medium onions, in ½-inch dice	1 cup banana flowers, rinsed (or dried lily flowers rinsed and soaked for 20 minutes)
6 fresh bay leaves (or 8 dried bay leaves)	⅛ cup fermented black beans	
	2 cups Shaoxing rice wine	
5 lbs pork belly, skin removed, in 3-inch cubes	1 cup Filipino soy sauce	

CHEF FINEZA is known as one of Vancouver's most adventurous chefs, from her fusion fare at Bin 942 to her pan-Asian dishes at Flying Tiger. Her French culinary training and Filipino heritage plus her ability to blend in Southeast Asian spices and cooking techniques have helped her redefine Pacific Northwest cuisine. Now a full-time restaurant consultant, she dedicates her time to creating recipes and inspiring new restaurants.

Humba is a Filipino term for slow-braised pork belly, and it's a favourite Filipino dish for party gatherings and special occasions. What makes this classic dish so authentic are ingredients such as fermented black beans, cane or coconut vinegar, Filipino soy sauce (made with added caramel) and banana flowers. These first three items can easily be found in Filipino markets, but banana flowers can be much harder to track down. Substitute dried lily flowers, which are available year-round in Chinese markets. Serve the pork with steamed long-grain white rice.

MAKE A SPICE sachet by placing a 6-inch square piece of cheesecloth on a clean work surface. Arrange the star anise, chilies, peppercorns and bay leaves in the middle of the cheesecloth. Gather the corners of the cheesecloth, completely encasing the spices, and tie tightly with a piece of kitchen twine. (Alternatively, use a store-bought fish or herb bag instead of a cheesecloth to hold the spices.) Set aside.

Heat a large braising pan (or a Dutch oven) on high, add pork belly and sear for 3 minutes. Turn pork over and sear for 3 minutes more, then repeat on all other sides until pork is completely browned. Set aside.

To the pan, add garlic, ginger, onions and black beans and sauté for 5 minutes. Slowly pour in wine and bring to a gentle boil. Reduce the heat to low. Add pork belly, spice sachet, soy sauce, vinegar, brown sugar and 2 to 3 cups water or enough to cover the pork belly. Bring to a boil, still on low heat, then reduce the heat to a simmer and braise for 2 hours.

Stir in banana flowers (or rehydrated lily flowers) and braise for another hour or until pork is fork-tender. Serve hot, directly from the pot.

STIR-FRIED SMOKED PORK

with Fresh Bamboo Shoots

Serves 4

BRINED, SMOKED PORK	8 oz pork belly, skinned	2 Tbsp black tea leaves
3 Tbsp salt	10 whole star anise	2 Tbsp uncooked long-grain rice
2 Tbsp + 2 tsp brown sugar	2 tsp whole cloves	
3 tsp Szechuan peppercorns	2 tsp fennel seeds	

HUNAN CUISINE is all about spices and intense flavour, and the award-winning Alvin Garden is justly famous for its very exotic, spicy and homestyle Hunan cooking. Be sure to try its celebrated pork and ginger soup, pork heart with five spices and the extra-hot boiled sliced beef with chili sauce.

Smoking is a traditional Hunan cooking technique used to preserve both meat and vegetables. It's also a palate-pleasing method, for it adds depth to the taste and texture of the food. This recipe involves brining the pork belly overnight and smoking it, which you can do ahead of time. Store the smoked meat in a sealed plastic bag or container and refrigerate it until ready to use. If you can't or don't want to smoke your own pork, substitute five-spice Chinese bacon (lap yok), which is available in most Chinese meat shops.

BRINED, SMOKED PORK Place 2 to 3 cups water in a medium pot; stir in salt, 2 tsp brown sugar and 1 tsp of the peppercorns. Bring to a boil on high heat and immediately turn off the stove. Remove from the heat and allow to cool completely. (The brine must be cold before adding the meat; otherwise, the heat would shock the meat and make it tough.)

Once cooled, transfer brine to a large plastic or glass container with a lid, and add pork belly, ensuring the meat is completely immersed. Discard excess brine. Cover and refrigerate overnight or for at least 12 hours.

To make a smoker, line both the inside of a 14-inch metal wok and its lid with heavy-duty aluminum foil, allowing at least 2 inches to hang over the edges.

Place the remaining 2 Tbsp brown sugar and 2 tsp peppercorns in the bottom of the wok with star anise, cloves, fennel seeds, tea leaves and rice. Set the rack in the middle position and preheat the wok on low.

Remove pork from the brine, rinse it and pat dry. Discard the brine. Place pork on the rack in the wok and increase the heat to medium. Cover the wok with the lid, ensuring the excess foil from the wok and the lid hang over the outside of the pot. Seal the edges by folding the foil together. (Start at one point, then turn the wok to fold the foil all the way around the pot, leaving only a 1-inch section unfolded to allow steam to escape.) When the sealing is done, remove the lid, leaving the top piece of

STIR FRY WITH FRESH BAMBOO SHOOTS

8 oz brined, smoked pork (or 8 oz packaged five-spice Chinese bacon [lap yok]) in ¹⁄₁₆-inch slices

2 cloves garlic, sliced

2 green onions, white and green parts, in 2-inch lengths

4 to 8 whole dried red chili peppers

1 tsp sesame oil

6 oz fresh young bamboo shoots, halved and sliced

½ green bell pepper, julienned

½ red bell pepper, julienned

1 tsp dark soy sauce

½ tsp brown sugar

foil in its place as the cover. Reduce the heat to medium-low and smoke pork for 40 minutes. Turn off the heat and allow to stand for 15 minutes.

Unseal the foil, remove the pork from the wok and set aside. Using oven mitts, remove the rack, then discard the spices and the foil. Wipe the wok clean with a wet towel.

STIR FRY WITH FRESH BAMBOO SHOOTS Heat the same wok on medium. Add pork (or bacon) and brown until meat starts to crisp up, about 10 minutes. Using a spoon, transfer pork (or bacon) to a medium bowl and set aside. Reserve the fat in the wok.

Add garlic, green onions and chili peppers and cook for about 90 seconds, or until they sizzle. Pour in sesame oil, then stir in bamboo shoots and pork (or bacon) and sauté for 30 seconds. Add red and green bell peppers, season with soy sauce and brown sugar, stir and cook for another 30 seconds. Serve immediately.

Fresh bamboo shoots

ROASTED CRISPY-SKIN PORK

Serves 8 to 10

5 lbs pork belly, skin attached	3 Tbsp white vinegar	4 oz maltose
6 tsp white sugar	1 Tbsp red rice vinegar	2 Tbsp oyster sauce
2 tsp salt	1 Tbsp Shaoxing rice wine	2 Tbsp brown bean sauce
2 Tbsp five-spice powder	4 oz mei gui lu (rose essence Chinese cooking wine)	1 Tbsp hoisin sauce
2 Tbsp ground lesser galangal (or ginger)		1 tsp Worcestershire sauce

THE ORIGINAL recipe, which is meant for a 40-pound suckling pig, involves Chef Hung turning and roasting the pig by hand over an open fire for the finishing touch. He has modified this recipe for home cooking. Although this dish seems to require almost a half a day to make, the actual preparation and baking times are very manageable. And the end result is definitely worth the effort!

Look for small packets of ground lesser galangal in the spice aisle, maltose in jars in the sugar aisle and jars or cans of brown bean sauce in the sauce aisle of Asian markets.

IN A MEDIUM stockpot, bring pork belly and 10 cups water to a boil on high heat. Reduce the heat to medium and boil for 45 minutes. Transfer pork to a large container and place under cold running water until pork is cold to the touch. Remove from the water, drain and pat dry.

In a small bowl, combine 3 tsp of the sugar, salt, five-spice powder and galangal (or ginger). Using your hands, rub this mixture evenly over the pork. Place pork on a platter and allow to rest for 40 minutes. In a medium saucepan, combine white vinegar, red rice vinegar, Shaoxing wine, mei gui lu wine and maltose. Bring to a boil on medium-low, then remove from the heat.

Rinse pork under running water, pat dry with paper towels and brush evenly with the vinegar-wine mixture. Allow to rest on a wire rack at room temperature for 3 hours. Reserve the remaining vinegar-wine mixture in the saucepan.

Preheat the oven to 375°F. Place pork, skin side up, on a greased wire rack set inside a baking pan. With a dessert fork, poke 2 or 3 columns of 4 to 6 rows of tiny holes in the pork skin. This allows air to escape from the meat and makes the skin crunchy. Bake for 90 minutes, basting pork with the remaining vinegar-wine mixture every 20 minutes until it is used up.

Before removing baked pork from the oven, increase the heat to broil and bake for 6 to 8 minutes until skin turns reddish brown. Remove from the oven and set aside to cool for 10 minutes.

In a small saucepan, bring oyster sauce, bean sauce, hoisin sauce, Worcestershire sauce, the remaining 3 tsp sugar and 2 Tbsp water to a gentle boil on medium heat. Stir and cook for 30 seconds, then remove from the heat. This is the dipping sauce. Transfer to a large sauce bowl.

Chop pork into bite-size pieces, transfer to a large platter and serve with dipping sauce.

ACROSS NORTH America, Asian greens such as gai lan (Chinese broccoli) and bok choy are now as easy to find as eggplants and shiitake mushrooms. Vegetables and starches are an essential complement to the seafood and meat dishes at any Asian meal, and vegetarianism is common in India and Taiwan and among Buddhists throughout Asia. Simply blanching or stir-frying vegetables is by far the most popular way to enjoy them: try the Mango Pepper Potatoes, which combines fruit and vegetables, or the Broad Bean Mash with Pickled Cabbage, which pairs two vegetables—one crunchy, one soft.

No meal is complete without a bowl of steamed rice, a tangle of noodles or a freshly baked flatbread to soak up sauces, temper fiery spices and add bulk to various dishes. Every region and culture has its own noodles made from starchy grains, roots, beans and legumes that are milled, mixed with water and sliced or pulled into long strands. Noodles are a must for Chinese birthday meals, since they symbolize longevity. Try them stir-fried with seafood and vegetables in Pad Thai or added to soups like Original Shanghai Tan Tan Noodles.

Rice—long- or short-grained, fragrant or wild—is stuffed into bamboo tubes and cooked over open fires in Malaysia, wrapped in lotus leaves and steamed in Thailand and China, baked with milk, sugar and spices in India. Sample the traditional Hainanese Chicken Rice, which is popular in Singapore and Malaysia, and Preserved Sausage Sandpot Rice, a mix of savoury meats cooked in a clay pot with a layer of slightly crunchy rice.

VEGETABLES, RICE AND NOODLES

SPICY ASIAN EGGPLANTS

Serves 4

½ cup chopped shallots

2 tsp chili paste

4 Tbsp vegetable oil

1 tsp shrimp paste

2 cloves garlic, crushed

¼ tsp salt

2 medium Asian eggplants,
in ½- × 1 ½-inch pieces

1 Tbsp brown sugar

1 tsp fresh lime juice

CHEF PHUA, formerly of Banana Leaf Malaysian Cuisine in Vancouver, has been luring fans of his award-winning Malaysian food to this inspired restaurant in New Westminster since 2006. This simple, delicious dish uses Asian eggplants, often sold as Japanese eggplants, which are longer and slimmer with a less woody texture than their Indian counterparts. A close relative of tomatoes and potatoes, these violet berry fruits are one of the essential vegetables of Southeast Asian cooking. Serve these eggplants over steamed jasmine rice or with roti, or any other flatbread, on the side.

PLACE SHALLOTS, CHILI paste, 2 Tbsp vegetable oil, shrimp paste, garlic and salt into a food processor and pulse for 2 to 3 minutes until the mixture becomes a paste.

In a wok, heat the remaining 2 Tbsp vegetable oil on medium-high. Reduce the heat to medium, add eggplants and cook for 3 minutes. Transfer eggplants to a large bowl, cover and set aside. Reduce the heat to low.

Stir in the shallot-chili paste and sauté for 1 minute. Increase the heat to high, then add eggplants, ¼ cup water, brown sugar and lime juice and stir well. Cover and cook for 3 to 4 minutes. Serve hot.

Asian eggplant

WOK-FRIED SPICY GREEN BEANS

Serves 4

5 Tbsp vegetable oil	¼ tsp salt
1 lb green beans, rinsed and dried	½ tsp white sugar
1 tsp minced garlic	1 Tbsp chopped green onions, white and green parts
1 Tbsp chili bean sauce	

IN A WOK, heat vegetable oil on high. Carefully add green beans, using a spatula to spread them evenly across the bottom of the pan. Pan-fry beans for 3 minutes, then turn them over and cook for 2 minutes more, or until tender. Using tongs, transfer beans to a plate.

To the wok, add garlic and sauté for 45 seconds until golden brown. Stir in green beans, chili bean sauce, salt and sugar and stir-fry for 2 to 3 minutes. Sprinkle with green onions. Transfer to a large serving platter and serve immediately.

THIS VERSATILE dish sometimes appears on menus at Mandarin restaurants as *gan bian si ji dou* and refers to the common Chinese cooking technique of flash-frying ingredients in hot oil to seal in the moisture and crisp the skin. Crispy on the outside and seasoned with chili bean sauce, this green bean dish is by far the most-often ordered vegetable course in Mandarin restaurants. Serve it with a bowl of steamed plain rice or vegetable noodle soup, or as part of a family-style meal.

Chinese long green beans

BROAD BEAN MASH
with Pickled Cabbage

Serves 4

12 oz peeled broad beans
(thawed if frozen)

1 tsp vegetable oil

1 can (200 g) pickled cabbage,
rinsed, drained and finely chopped

1 tsp white sugar

1 tsp sesame oil

BROAD BEANS (also known as large fava beans) are low in fat but high in protein and minerals and are common in many Asian and African regions. In China, they are cooked as a meal, as a side dish or as a snack—and even for medicinal purposes. This nutritious bean recipe is popular in northern Guangdong, where it's a favoured and nutritious vegetarian dish. Look for canned pickled cabbage, which is actually brined and pickled Chinese mustard (*shi-li-hon*) in Asian groceries, and substitute peas if you can't find prepackaged peeled broad beans. For this recipe, cook the broad beans in a ceramic or other nonreactive pot, as a stainless steel or iron pot will blacken them.

PLACE BEANS IN a medium pot and add enough water to cover beans by 1 inch. Cover and bring to a boil on high heat, then reduce the heat to medium and cook for 5 minutes. Reduce the heat to low and simmer for about 45 minutes or until water starts to dry up and beans become tender. (Check halfway through cooking and add more water if necessary.) Allow beans to drain in a colander for 5 minutes, then transfer to a medium bowl. Mash beans for 3 to 4 minutes until they are smooth like mashed potatoes and set aside.

Heat vegetable oil in a wok on high. Add pickled cabbage and sugar and sauté for 2 to 3 minutes. Reduce the heat to medium-low. Stir in mash, mix well to combine and sauté for 3 to 4 minutes. Add sesame oil and season to taste with salt and freshly ground black pepper. Serve immediately or allow to cool for 20 to 30 minutes and serve warm.

CHINESE CABBAGE IN DASHI BROTH
(Hakusai Nibitashi)
Serves 4

one 3-inch square kombu

5 Tbsp shaved dry bonito flakes

8 pieces deep-fried tofu,
each 1¼ inches thick

2 Tbsp mirin

2 Tbsp light soy sauce

10 oz Chinese cabbage

1 Tbsp vegetable oil

1 tsp sesame oil

1 tsp black sesame seeds

IN A SMALL pot combine kombu and 2 cups water, and heat on medium-high for 3 to 4 minutes. Before water comes to a boil, turn off the heat and remove and discard the kombu. Add 4 Tbsp of the bonito flakes and allow to steep for 5 minutes.

Place a fine-mesh sieve over a small bowl. Strain broth, discarding bonito flakes and any other solids. This broth is called dashi.

In a medium saucepan, bring 2 cups water to a boil on high heat. Add tofu and blanch for 1 minute, then, using a slotted spoon, transfer to a colander to drain.

In a medium pot, combine dashi, mirin and soy sauce and bring to a gentle boil on medium-high heat. Turn off the heat.

Using a sharp knife, cut cabbage into 1½-inch lengths. Separate stems and leaves into 2 piles. In a large frying pan, heat vegetable oil on high. Add cabbage stems and sauté for 1 minute. Add sesame oil and cook for 30 seconds. Stir in cabbage leaves and tofu and mix well. Pour in the dashi mixture and bring to a gentle boil, then season with salt to taste. Remove from the heat. (If you plan to serve this as a cold dish, allow the frying pan to cool slightly, then place it in a large roasting pan. Fill the roasting pan ½ full with ice water and set aside for 15 to 20 minutes.) Transfer to a deep serving bowl and garnish with sesame seeds and the remaining 1 Tbsp bonito flakes.

SHURAKU, LOCATED on busy, trendy Granville Street, is best described as an izakaya-meets-bistro, a spot where Chef Omori creates familiar Japanese dishes with a West Coast touch. Every dish is beautifully plated, and the attention to detail is evident in every bite. This is also a great place to sample from an extensive sake menu.

Nibitashi is a popular Japanese dish that refers to sautéing food, then boiling it in dashi. Vegetables are usually the main ingredients, including this version made with hakusai (also known as Chinese cabbage or siu choy), but sometimes seafood is added. Serve hot, cold or at room temperature as an appetizer or a side dish.

EASILY ACCESSIBLE FROM downtown Vancouver by Sky-Train is North Burnaby's Asian hub, Metrotown Mall. It's home to T&T Supermarket, the busiest and most concentrated centre of Asian eat-in or take-out food in the city. First opened in 1993, this store's food department is a cornucopia of cooking stations for Chinese barbecue and other foods, take-out display cases for sushi and Asian deli items, beverage stations and a full-service bakery. Be sure to visit the adjacent cafeteria, where the smells of soy and sizzle emanate from the many hot and cold ready-made dishes of Korean, Japanese, Taiwanese and Chinese food, including many daily specials. Also worth a stop in the mall is Dessert Dynasty, the first bubble tea café in Metro Vancouver, an open-style café that will lure you in with its delicious aromas of freshly made bubble teas, crêpes and egg-bubble waffles.

Around the corner from Metrotown is Crystal Mall, the only exclusively Asian shopping complex in Burnaby. Join the steady stream of shoppers filing in and out of the centre's huge Chinese market, then line up in the busy food court for Wang's juicy pork dumplings, or stop at Top Gun Hot Pot, where fine Chinese tea is served in old-style individual teacups. On the ground floor several ethnic restaurants, including a typical Hong Kong–style café called Pittsburg that offers a multitude of Asian dishes as well as Western-style plates such as steaks and pork chops, are popular lunchtime haunts, as are a concentration of restaurants along nearby Kingsway. Here, you find groups of students grabbing a quick meal at Sushi Garden or business-people talking on their cellphones and wolfing down Lao Shan Dong's homemade noodles or Saffron Indian Cuisine's tantalizing vegetable paneer pakoras. In the evening the pace is slower, as families and young couples relax over their meals in restaurants from Willingdon Street to Royal Oak Avenue.

MANGO PEPPER POTATOES

Serves 4

1 Tbsp coriander seeds	4 Tbsp ghee (or vegetable oil)	1 medium onion, grated
4 whole pods black cardamom	1 lb nugget potatoes, peeled and quartered	½ tsp turmeric
2 whole pods green cardamom		1 tsp chili powder
4 to 5 whole cloves	4 to 5 bay leaves	½ cup milk
7 to 8 black peppercorns	pinch of asafoetida (optional)	2 cups peeled and diced mango
1 small stick cinnamon	1 tsp ginger-garlic paste	½ tsp freshly ground black pepper
¼ tsp caraway seeds		

IN A SPICE/COFFEE grinder, grind coriander, black and green cardamom, cloves, peppercorns, cinnamon and caraway to a fine powder. This is the garam masala, or spice mix, for this recipe.

In a large frying pan, heat 2 Tbsp of the ghee (or vegetable oil) on medium. Add potatoes and sauté for 4 to 5 minutes, or until light brown. Transfer to a bowl and set aside.

Increase the heat to medium-high. Return the pan to the stove and add the remaining 2 Tbsp ghee (or vegetable oil). Stir in bay leaves, asafoetida, ginger-garlic paste and onions and sauté for 5 to 8 minutes, or until brownish. Stir in garam masala and sauté for 2 to 3 minutes, then add turmeric, chili powder and salt to taste and sauté for another minute. Gently pour in milk and mango, mix well and simmer for 2 minutes, stirring continuously. If the sauce becomes too thick, like the consistency of gravy, add ¼ cup water.

Add potatoes, stirring well to coat them, then cook for 8 to 10 minutes, or until potatoes are tender. Season with black pepper and serve in a large serving bowl.

IN INDIA, where there are over one hundred varieties of mango, this fruit, one of the country's national foods, plays an important role both in agriculture and in the kitchen. Mango chutneys and relishes and mango beverages are familiar recipes, but incorporating ripe mango pulp, potatoes and a multitude of traditional Indian herbs and spices into a vegetarian entrée takes this juicy fruit to a whole new level. Choose large Filipino mangoes for this recipe, and look for ginger-garlic paste in Indian markets. Serve this dish with basmati rice, naan or chapattis.

BRAISED KAOFU

with Mushrooms, Wood Ears and Bamboo Shoots

Serves 6 to 8

8 medium Chinese dried black mushrooms (or fresh shiitakes)

2 oz wood ear fungus

1 oz dried lily buds, in 2-inch lengths

4 cups vegetable stock

1 oz rock sugar (or white sugar)

3 Tbsp soy sauce

2 Tbsp mushroom-flavoured dark soy sauce

1 Tbsp mushroom seasoning (optional)

1 lb kaofu, in ½- × 2-inch pieces

4 Tbsp vegetable oil

3 oz fresh bamboo shoots, in ⅟₁₆-inch slices

1 Tbsp sesame oil

KAOFU IS a steamed fluffy loaf made with wheat gluten, bread flour and baking powder. Its high protein content and sponge-cake texture make it the ideal meat replacement. Just like tofu, kaofu plays an indispensable role in Asian vegetarian cooking.

In Vancouver, there are only a handful of restaurants entirely devoted to vegetarian cooking, and Chef Fang's homestyle recipes are among the best. In addition to preparing food for her own patrons at Evergreen Vegetarian House, a tiny takeout location at the Empire Centre food court in Richmond, she supplies ready-made foods to a number of local Chinese restaurants. Chef Fang recommends Japanese sesame oil and Yamasa soy sauce, or another naturally fermented soy sauce, for this recipe. Mushroom seasoning can be found in bottles in the sauce and seasoning aisle in Asian markets.

SEPARATELY RINSE CHINESE mushrooms and wood ears thoroughly under running water. Fill 2 medium bowls with 2 cups water each, add mushrooms to one and wood ears to the other and soak for at least 1 hour, or until tender. Drain Chinese mushrooms, remove and discard stems and set aside. Then drain wood ears, slice into bite-size pieces, rinse again and set aside. Rinse lily buds under running water. Fill a small bowl with 2 cups water, add lily buds and soak for 15 to 20 minutes. Drain and set aside.

In a medium saucepan, bring 2 cups of the vegetable stock, sugar, soy sauce, dark soy sauce and mushroom seasoning to a gentle boil on medium. Remove from the heat and allow to cool for 20 to 30 minutes. Add kaofu. Using a spatula, toss kaofu in the marinade, pressing it to be sure liquid is evenly distributed. Set aside for 30 minutes.

Place a strainer over a medium bowl. Drain kaofu, reserving the marinade and pressing with the spatula to extract as much marinade as possible. Place kaofu in a separate bowl.

In a wok, heat 3 Tbsp of the vegetable oil on high. Add kaofu and sauté for 1 minute. Add marinade, stirring and cooking for 3 to 4 minutes, or until it's completely absorbed. Return kaofu to the bowl and set aside. Reduce the heat to medium.

Heat the remaining 1 Tbsp vegetable oil in the wok, then add Chinese mushrooms and sauté for 30 seconds. Increase the heat to high, add 1 cup of the vegetable stock, cover and cook for 2 minutes. Add bamboo shoots, stir well, then cover and cook for 2 to 3 minutes, or until stock is absorbed. Add the remaining 1 cup vegetable stock, wood ears and lily buds, mix well and bring to a gentle boil. Reduce the heat to low, add kaofu without stirring, and cover and cook for 2 to 3 minutes. Remove the lid and stir gently for 30 to 45 seconds, or until stock is fully absorbed.

Transfer to a large serving platter, drizzle evenly with sesame oil and serve immediately.

TOMATO RICE

Serves 6 to 8

1 Tbsp ghee (or canola oil)	1 medium red onion, finely sliced	½ tsp chili powder
1 tsp mustard seeds	1-inch-slice ginger, finely chopped	¼ tsp turmeric
1 tsp fennel seeds	2 cups chopped tomatoes	4 cups slightly undercooked basmati rice
1 tsp cumin seeds	2 green chili peppers, halved and seeded	½ chopped fresh cilantro
1 sprig curry leaves		

THIS HEARTY vegetarian one-pot wonder is the perfect meal for families and friendly get-togethers. Just add a salad or a soup of your choice for a full meal. Refrigerate any leftover tomato rice in an airtight container for up to 2 days. To serve, simply reheat it gently in the microwave.

IN A MEDIUM saucepan, heat ghee (or canola oil) on medium-high. Add mustard seeds, and when they start to pop, about 15 seconds, add fennel and cumin seeds and brown for 2 minutes. Stir in curry leaves, onions and ginger and cook for 4 to 5 minutes, until onions start to brown. Add tomatoes and chili peppers, cook for 2 minutes, then sprinkle in chili powder and turmeric. Cook for about 5 minutes until the mixture is well combined.

Add rice and stir well. Cover and cook for 15 minutes, or until rice fluffs up. Garnish with cilantro and serve immediately.

Curry leaves

SEAFOOD AND TOBIKO FRIED RICE

Serves 4

½ tsp salt

4 whole scallops, in ¾-inch dice

6 prawns, peeled, deveined
and cut in ¾-inch dice

3 oz sole fillet, in ¾-inch dice

3 cups cooked plain
long-grain white rice

3 Tbsp vegetable oil

4 medium eggs, beaten

2 tsp fish sauce

3 oz tobiko

1 green onion, chopped

1 tsp sesame oil

IN A LARGE pot, bring 3 cups water to a rolling boil on high heat. Add salt, scallops, prawns and sole and blanch for 45 seconds. Remove from the heat and transfer to a colander. Immediately rinse the seafood under cold running water to stop the cooking. Drain and set aside.

Place rice in a microwave-safe bowl and microwave for 90 seconds on high. Set aside.

In a wok, heat vegetable oil on high, add eggs and scramble for 15 to 20 seconds until semi-cooked. Add scallops, prawns and sole and sauté for 10 seconds only. Stir in rice and fish sauce and stir-fry for 1 minute. Add tobiko and green onions and mix well for 30 seconds. Pour in sesame oil, stirring constantly. Stir for another 10 seconds and serve immediately.

THAI IN THE VILLAGE is the first Asian bistro in Whistler to serve signature dishes from Thailand, Japan and neighbouring Asian regions. In this Japanese-meets-Cantonese rice dish, bright-orange tobiko, or flying fish roe, lends crunchiness and a briny flavour. Although it's less expensive to buy frozen tobiko in large packages from Asian markets, small boxes of fresh tobiko are available for home cooking. Serve this dish on its own as a main course or as part of a family-style meal.

HAINANESE CHICKEN RICE

Serves 4 to 6

1 whole chicken, about 3 lbs	6 cloves garlic + 4 Tbsp minced garlic	2 tsp white sugar
3½ tsp salt	4 Tbsp shallots, minced	3 green onions, chopped
15 slices ginger, each ⅟₁₆-inch thick	6 fresh red hot chili peppers, seeded and chopped	¼ English cucumber, thinly sliced
2 cups long-grain rice		2 sprigs fresh cilantro, in 2-inch lengths
2 Tbsp vegetable oil		

CHINESE SETTLERS from the island of Hainan and neighbouring regions brought the original Hainanese chicken recipe to Singapore and Malaysia around the turn of the twentieth century. It has since become a staple dish in these two countries. Here in Vancouver, almost every Singaporean or Malaysian restaurant serves Hainanese chicken, but this one from Café D'Lite is among the best. Although the recipe has two components—the chicken and the rice—restaurants often present the chicken, half or whole, as an entrée and the chicken rice as a side order. Luckily, some Hong Kong–style cafés do serve the two parts together as a set meal. Prepare the chicken an hour and a half before you cook the rice.

RINSE CHICKEN UNDER cold running water, pat dry with paper towels and trim off any excess fat.

In a large stockpot, bring 8 to 10 cups water (or enough to cover chicken), 2 tsp of the salt and 4 slices of the ginger to a boil on high heat. Add chicken, breast side down, and reduce the heat to minimum. Cover and simmer for 25 minutes. Using tongs, turn chicken over so it is back side down, cover and simmer for another 20 to 30 minutes. (To test for doneness, poke a knife into the thickest part of the breast. If the juices run clear, the chicken is cooked through.)

Transfer chicken to a large colander, reserving the cooking water to cook the rice, and set it under cold running water for 10 minutes to tighten the skin and tenderize the meat. Drain chicken, cover and allow to cool to room temperature.

Rinse rice with cold water and allow to drain in a colander for 10 to 15 minutes.

Heat a wok on high, then add vegetable oil, 2 Tbsp of the minced garlic, 2 Tbsp of the shallots and 3 slices of the ginger. Sauté for 3 to 4 minutes until garlic and shallots are golden. Add rice and sauté for another 3 to 4 minutes, then transfer to an electric rice cooker. Add 3 cups of the reserved chicken stock and 1 tsp of the salt. Cook rice according to the directions on the rice cooker.

While the rice is cooking, prepare the chili and ginger sauces. To make the chili sauce, place chili peppers, the remaining 2 Tbsp minced garlic and 2 Tbsp minced shallots, 3 slices of the ginger and 1 tsp sugar in a food processor. Blend for 2 to 3 minutes until the mixture forms a paste, then transfer it to a bowl. In a small microwave-safe bowl, heat 2 tsp reserved chicken stock in the microwave and add it to the paste. Place chili sauce in a sauce bowl and set aside.

To make the ginger sauce, place the remaining 5 slices ginger, 6 garlic cloves and green onions in a food processor and blend for 45 seconds. Transfer the mixture to a sauce bowl, then stir in 2 tsp reserved chicken stock, the remaining ½ tsp salt and 1 tsp sugar. Set aside.

To serve, chop chicken into bite-size pieces (deboning is optional) and arrange on a platter. Garnish with cucumber and cilantro. Mound chicken rice in a large serving bowl. Serve, family-style, with chili sauce and ginger sauce on the side.

PRESERVED SAUSAGE SANDPOT RICE

Serves 2

1 cup long-grain rice, rinsed

1 Chinese lean pork sausage, rinsed and cut in ⅛-inch diagonal slices

1 Chinese pork and chicken liver sausage, rinsed and cut in ⅛-inch diagonal slices

2 oz preserved Chinese pork (lap yok), in ¹⁄₁₆-inch slices

½ tsp vegetable oil

4 to 6 stalks baby bok choy, rinsed

1 Tbsp dark soy sauce

1 Tbsp light soy sauce

1 tsp white sugar

1 tsp sesame oil

1 Tbsp chopped green onion, white and green parts

1 Tbsp chopped fresh cilantro

THE FOOD COURT of a shopping mall may not sound like a promising place to find great Asian food, but James Snacks is well worth a visit. It's the only place in Metro Vancouver to find takeout sandpot rice, and its made-to-order pots of rice have earned the restaurant many accolades and repeat visitors.

In the old days before electric rice cookers, rice was cooked either in a wok or in a clay pot (sand pot). Now claypot rice has become a specialty course. The key to a great pot of rice is attention and timing: watch the pot of rice as it cooks so that you can properly time the cooking process. To enjoy crispy rice cracklings, the bottom layer of semi-burnt rice, leave the rice on the heat for an extra 3 to 4 minutes. Chinese clay pots can be purchased in any Chinese supermarket or Chinese cookware store.

IN AN 8-INCH Chinese clay pot, combine rice and about 1¼ cups of water (enough water to cover rice by ½ inch). Cook on medium-high, covered, for 5 to 7 minutes until water bubbles up. Remove the lid and stir a few times with a spoon. Arrange sausages and preserved pork on top of the rice, reduce the heat to low, cover and cook for 20 to 25 minutes or until pork fat becomes almost translucent.

While the sausages are cooking, place 2 cups water in a small pot and bring to a boil on high heat. Add vegetable oil and baby bok choy. Cover and cook for 90 seconds, then remove from the heat and drain bok choy in a colander. In the same pot, combine dark and light soy sauces, sugar, sesame oil and 1 Tbsp water on medium heat and bring to a gentle boil. Stir and cook for 15 seconds, then turn off the heat.

Place green onions and cilantro in a small serving bowl, then pour the soy mixture over it. Serve rice and sausages in the pot, family-style, garnish with bok choy and pass around the soy mixture as a condiment.

WOK-FRIED VERMICELLI
with Mushrooms and Bean Sprouts
Serves 4

3 Tbsp vegetable oil

1 pkg (454 g) dried
vermicelli noodles

1 pkg (200 g) fresh enoki
mushrooms

1 Tbsp chopped ginger

1 medium yellow onion, julienned

4 shiitake mushrooms, julienned

4 crimini mushrooms, sliced

2 Tbsp dark soy sauce

2 Tbsp light soy sauce

1 tsp white sugar

8 oz bean sprouts

3 green onions, julienned

IN A MEDIUM stockpot, bring 8 cups water to a full boil on high heat. Add 1 Tbsp of the vegetable oil and the vermicelli and return to a boil. Reduce the heat to low, cover and cook for 3 minutes. Remove the pot from the heat and allow to sit for 5 minutes. Drain noodles in a colander and set aside.

Trim and discard 1½ inches from the bottom of enoki mushrooms and separate them by hand.

In a wok, bring the remaining 2 Tbsp vegetable oil to a boil on high heat. Add ginger and onions and brown for 30 seconds. Stir in enoki, shiitake and crimini mushrooms and sauté for 1 minute. Add vermicelli and sauté for 2 minutes. Stir in dark and light soy sauces and sugar, and cook for another 2 minutes. Add bean sprouts and green onions and sauté for 1 minute more.

To crisp some of the vermicelli, cover and cook for 3 to 4 minutes. Serve immediately, sizzling hot, on a large family-style platter.

MUSHROOMS OF any kind are virtually essential ingredients for flavourful Asian vegetarian dishes, including noodle courses. Although the ginger and green onions deliver the enticing base flavour, it's the wok energy—the umami flavour derived from quick-cooking foods over high heat—that puts the sizzle in this dish.

Use rice or mung bean vermicelli to make this recipe. To add colour or vary the flavour, you can add other vegetables such as carrots and snow peas.

INDIANS OWN AND work much of the farmland and many of the orchards in Surrey and Langley. They supply grocery stores and restaurants across the Lower Mainland and often sell their produce at the farm gate.

Closer to town, Scott Road (120 Street) is still home to the largest concentration of Indian grocery stores and Indian eateries, where the large Indian population in Surrey and the surrounding area do their shopping and entertaining. As you drive along this bustling road, you can find standout restaurants such as Mahek Restaurant and Lounge (voted number 1 in Surrey and Delta) and Mehfil India Restaurant (Surrey's largest Indian buffet). The newly opened Ashiana Dil Kash Cuisine, the sister restaurant of Ashiana Tandoori, is a banquet hall situated right next to the area's largest South Asian supermarket, Fruiticana's flagship store at the corner of 120 Street and 80th Avenue.

Asian Spice, which serves Indian-style Chinese and Szechuan food, is one of the smaller-scale family-style Indian restaurants scattered along the same corridor. As well, the two-foot-long dosa and the twelve-item thali served at Desi Dosa Madras Restaurant are must-tries. Take a beverage break at the state-of-the-art bar inside the modern and cozy Desi Junction Bar and Restaurant located at the other end of the same strip mall. In any of these eateries, you're likely to find women dressed in beautiful saris sitting side-by-side with their kids who are wearing the latest skinny jeans and fitted shirts, all of them set against a backdrop of large plasma TVs playing the newest Bollywood musical.

Many Indian businesses have opened on 128th Street, making this a very busy strip. A few notable eateries have followed suit: the coveted Chili Pepper House, which serves Indian-style Chinese food in its seventies-style dining room, flanks the corner of 128th Street and 96th Avenue, and Yellow Chilli Restaurant and Bar, which specializes in traditional North Indian dishes, occupies the intersection of 128th Street and 72nd Avenue. Several strip malls, some with colossal Indian banquet halls extending across their second floors, are also dominant on 128th Street.

During the week, these are the lunch rooms for delivery drivers, neighbourhood workers and businesspeople. On the weekends, however, the restaurants come alive as family gathering spots. Men in elaborately embroidered sherwanis and kurtas and women in rainbow-coloured, sequined saris or lehengas dance to trendy Indian music while overflowing plates of catered food make sure no one goes home hungry.

Unless you're lucky enough to be invited to a banquet or a family home, other good places to look for authentic Indian food are the places that cater the buffets served in those banquet halls: Gulberg Fine Cuisine on Fraser Highway, which has many Pakistani specialties, and Dakshin Indian Cuisine on King George Highway, which focusses more on South Indian dishes. Lovely Sweet Shop and Restaurant is also a good bet for takeout meals.

MALAYSIAN SPICY PAN MEE NOODLES

Serves 4

1 lb ground pork

1½ tsp salt

2 tsp freshly ground black pepper

3 tsp light soy sauce

1 tsp cornstarch

2 to 3 Tbsp dried chili flakes, rinsed, soaked and drained

1 to 2 red hot chili peppers, or to taste

4 shallots, chopped

1 cup + 8 tsp vegetable oil

1 lb fresh flat flour noodles (or Shanghai noodles or fettuccine)

2 tsp oyster sauce

4 Tbsp dried anchovies

¼ tsp white sugar

1 large egg

4 green onions, white and green parts, chopped

IN MALAYSIA, pan mee noodles are consumed throughout the day—at any meal or even as a snack—which is a good indication of just how cherished this spicy dish is. *Pan mee* literally means "flat flour noodles," and they are offered fried with sauces and condiments or in soup form.

This very spicy version is from Café D'Lite, an unassuming little family-run eatery that's been around for 20 years. Chef Lee's wholesome cooking is reminiscent of a mother's home cooking, but the plates are nicely presented. Definitely cheap and cheerful, Café D'Lite is famous for its Hainanese Chicken Rice (page 170) and its dessert soups. The restaurant also sells its own sauces in jars.

Look for packaged fresh flat flour noodles in the cooler aisle of Asian supermarkets and Chinese noodle shops.

IN A LARGE bowl, combine pork with ½ tsp of the salt, 1 tsp of the black pepper, 1 tsp of the soy sauce and cornstarch until well mixed. Set aside.

In a food processor, combine dried and fresh chili peppers, half of the shallots, ½ tsp of the salt, ½ tsp of the black pepper and 3 tsp of the vegetable oil. Pulse for 20 to 30 seconds.

In a wok, heat 1 cup vegetable oil on medium-low. Add the chili mixture and fry for about 2 minutes, or until golden brown. Remove from the heat, drain the oil into an airtight container and transfer the chili mixture into a bowl to use as a condiment. (The chili oil will keep, refrigerated, for up to 4 weeks.)

In a large pot, boil 10 cups water. Add noodles, cover and cook for 4 to 5 minutes or until water boils again. Reduce the heat to low, cover and cook for 2 to 3 minutes. Remove the pot from the heat and set aside for 5 to 7 minutes. Drain the noodles, then transfer to a large serving platter.

In the wok, heat 2 tsp of the vegetable oil on high. Add the remaining shallots and sauté for 20 seconds. Stir in ground pork and stir-fry for 4 to 6 minutes, or until cooked. Pour in the remaining 2 tsp soy sauce, oyster sauce and ½ cup water, stir and cook for 2 minutes. Season with the remaining ½ tsp salt and ½ tsp black pepper, then pour the pork mixture over the noodles.

To the wok, add the remaining 3 tsp vegetable oil and heat on high. Add anchovies and fry for 60 seconds until golden. Stir in sugar and add to the platter.

In a small saucepan, boil 1 cup water on high. Crack egg into the water, turn off the heat, cover and allow to rest for 5 minutes. Using a slotted spoon, remove the egg and add it to the platter. Garnish with 1 tsp of the chili mixture and green onions. Serve immediately.

PAD THAI

Serves 3 to 4

1 lb Thai rice noodles	2 large eggs, beaten	3 Tbsp tamarind sauce
½ cup canola oil	1 Tbsp fish sauce	1 cup bean sprouts
1 Tbsp minced garlic	1 Tbsp palm sugar	2 Tbsp roasted peanuts, crushed
10 medium prawns, peeled and deveined	1 Tbsp tomato paste	½ lime, in 4 wedges

THANKS TO tamarind sauce, tangy pad Thai is the single-most notable Thai noodle dish and a must-have item on every Thai restaurant menu. In fact, pad Thai was introduced from Vietnam around the 1930s and started as a simple, convenient meal made by mixing noodles with whatever ingredients were on hand. This comfort food now has many versions, depending on the time of the day and what's available.

Authentic pad Thai has no ketchup in it, though some chefs add a touch of tomato paste. Traditionally any sweetness came from the tamarind. In North America, tamarind is now widely available in Asian markets and grocery stores, as fresh tamarind pods or as vacuum-sealed packages of fresh shelled tamarind or as jars of prepared tamarind sauce. For the best results, make your own tamarind sauce by soaking fresh tamarind pulp in hot water (use half as much water as there is pulp) and mix well when softened.

FILL A LARGE bowl with 10 to 12 cups water and set aside for 15 to 20 minutes to allow it to come to room temperature. Add noodles and soak for 20 to 30 minutes or until softened. Drain in a colander.

In a wok, heat canola oil on high, add garlic and sizzle for 30 seconds or until golden brown. Add prawns and sauté for 30 seconds until orange-red, then add eggs and stir quickly for 15 seconds until lightly scrambled. Stir in noodles, sauté for 2 to 3 minutes, then add fish sauce, sugar, tomato paste and tamarind sauce. Stir well and cook for 3 to 4 minutes, then transfer the noodles to a large serving bowl. Garnish with bean sprouts and peanuts. Arrange lime wedges on a plate and serve on the side. Serve immediately.

ORIGINAL SHANGHAI TAN TAN NOODLES

Serves 2

½ tsp vegetable oil

1 tsp salt

10 oz fresh Shanghai noodles
(or 8 oz dried Shanghai noodles)

3 Tbsp minced garlic

4 Tbsp sesame paste

3 Tbsp dark soy sauce

2 Tbsp light soy sauce

2 to 3 Tbsp red chili oil

4 Tbsp Szechuan preserved
vegetables, rinsed, drained
and finely chopped

3 cups vegetable stock

3 Tbsp chopped green onions,
white and green parts

IN A MEDIUM saucepan, bring 6 cups water to a boil on high heat. Add vegetable oil, ½ tsp of the salt and the noodles and bring to a boil again. If using fresh noodles, boil for 3 to 4 minutes; for dried noodles, boil for 6 to 8 minutes, stirring halfway through the cooking time. Turn off the heat and allow to rest for 2 to 3 minutes, or until noodles are cooked al dente (soft but not mushy). Drain noodles in a colander and divide them into 2 large serving bowls.

In a medium bowl, combine the remaining ½ tsp salt, garlic, sesame paste, dark and light soy sauces, chili oil and preserved vegetables. Scatter evenly over the noodles in the 2 bowls.

In a medium saucepan, bring vegetable stock to a full boil on high heat. Carefully pour the hot stock directly onto the sauce in each bowl. Garnish with green onions and serve immediately.

TAN TAN (also called *dan dan*) noodles, a regional meatless meal from Szechuan and Shanghai, are as well known and widely revered as Cantonese won ton noodle soup. The name *tan tan* refers to the long, thick bamboo pole called *danzi* that roving hawkers used to sell their wares in nearby neighbourhoods in the early days. Balanced on each end of the pole, which the hawkers slung across their shoulders, were two small wooden carts containing bowls, a pot of steaming homemade soup, ready-to-toss noodles and a savoury sauce.

This version is from the restaurant many consider to be the best noodle house in Vancouver. Lin Chef Zhang and Dim Sum Chef Miao have been featured on numerous local and international television programs and are lauded for their exceptional *xiao long bao* (steamed dumplings) and noodle dishes.

This recipe calls for Szechuan preserved vegetables, which are brined and chili-spiced mustard green stems. They're available in Asian markets in cans, in vacuum packs or loosely stacked in large pots.

SAUTÉED BEEF HOR FAN
with Prawns, Bean Sprouts and XO Sauce
Serves 3 to 4

4 oz beef tenderloin,
very thinly sliced

½ tsp + 4 Tbsp canola oil

½ green bell pepper, julienned

½ red bell pepper, julienned

2 oz bean sprouts

4 prawns, peeled, deveined
and patted dried

1 lb fresh hor fan noodles,
separated by hand

½ tsp dark soy sauce

¼ tsp sugar

1 Tbsp XO sauce

1 tsp white sesame seeds

2 Tbsp coarsely chopped
fresh cilantro

IN A MEDIUM bowl, toss beef slices with ½ tsp canola oil until well coated. (This step helps to soften the meat slices and makes it easier to fry them.) Set aside.

Bring 2 cups water to a boil in a wok on high heat. Blanch green and red bell peppers and sprouts for 1 minute. Using a slotted spoon, transfer vegetables to a colander to drain. Set vegetables aside and discard the water. Wipe the wok dry with a paper towel.

To the wok, add 1 Tbsp canola oil and carefully bring to a boil on high heat. Keeping your face away from the wok, gently add beef and fry for 30 seconds, without stirring. Using a turner, turn beef over and fry for another 30 seconds, then transfer to a plate. Add another 1 Tbsp canola oil and the prawns and fry for 30 to 40 seconds, or until they turn orange-red. Transfer to another plate and set aside.

Return the wok to high heat. When the wok starts smoking, add the remaining 2 Tbsp canola oil. Add noodles and sauté for 2 to 3 minutes, stirring constantly to prevent them from sticking. Stir in green and red bell peppers, sprouts, beef and prawns. Add soy sauce, sugar and XO sauce, mix well and cook for 2 minutes. Transfer to a large platter and garnish with sesame seeds and cilantro. Serve hot.

HON'S IS a Vancouver culinary icon. The oldest surviving won ton house in the city, Hon's original location opened in the centre of Chinatown in 1972, serving authentic Hong Kong–style noodles. Today, Hon's is a noodle factory, a Chinese food shop and four family-style restaurants that serve a wide range of traditional Chinese food. An institution, it continues to win awards for its casual Chinese fare, and its noodles are sold in major supermarkets across the region.

Hor fan are fresh, wide, snow-white noodles made by steaming fresh liquefied rice flour and are fluffy, tender and absorbent. They originated in eastern Guangdong, where the Hakka natives dwell. You can find fresh hor fan noodles and uncut sheets wrapped in plastic in the cooler section of Asian food stores and noodle shops; remove them from the package and separate them by hand before cooking them.

NOODLES WITH KIMCHI
in Dried Anchovy Broth
Serves 4 to 6

two bundles (from a 340-g pkg) ver-micelli coreen (Korean-style sweet potato starch noodles)

¼ cup dried anchovies

one 3-inch square kombu

3 tsp light soy sauce

2½ tsp white sugar

1 tsp salt

2¼ Tbsp vegetable oil

1 medium onion, thinly sliced

1 egg, beaten

4 oz beef tenderloin, julienned

½ tsp minced garlic

2½ tsp sesame oil

½ tsp freshly ground black pepper

one 2-inch square fried fish paste, julienned

¼ cup kimchi, squeezed by hand to remove excess liquid, in thin strips

1 Tbsp chopped green onions, white and green parts

MOST KOREAN noodles are made with flour from tubers such as potatoes and yams. These noodles are lighter and more elastic than traditional wheat or rice noodles, and they're translucent and less doughy when cooked. Korean markets are the best place to shop for these noodles and other Korean ingredients.

IN A MEDIUM pot, bring 6 cups water to a boil on high heat and add noodles. Boil for 4 to 5 minutes until translucent, then drain in a large colander. Rinse noodles under cold running water for 3 minutes, then set aside to drain again. Rinse the pot.

Add 6 cups cold water, dried anchovies and kombu and bring to a boil on high heat. Reduce the heat to low, cover and simmer for 8 minutes, then, using a slotted spoon, remove and discard anchovies and kombu. Skim and discard any impurities from the top of the broth. Add 2 tsp of the soy sauce, ½ tsp of the sugar and ½ tsp of the salt, then bring to a boil again and turn off the heat. Set aside.

In a small frying pan, heat 1 Tbsp of the vegetable oil on high. Add onions and sauté for 2 to 3 minutes until golden brown. Transfer to a small serving bowl and set aside.

To the frying pan, add ¼ Tbsp of the vegetable oil. Stir in egg and immediately reduce the heat to low. Swirl the pan to make an egg crêpe, and cook for 2 minutes. Transfer cooked egg to a plate, sprinkle with a pinch of salt and allow to cool for 3 minutes. Cut egg in ¼-inch strips and place in a small serving bowl.

In a small bowl, combine beef, ½ tsp of the soy sauce, ½ tsp of the sugar, garlic, ½ tsp of the sesame oil, the remaining ½ tsp salt and ¼ tsp of the black pepper. In the frying pan, heat the remaining 1 Tbsp vegetable oil on high, add beef and cook for 30 seconds. Turn beef over and cook for 30 seconds, then stir-fry for another 30 seconds and transfer to a serving bowl.

In a small saucepan, combine ½ tsp soy sauce, ½ tsp sugar and ¼ tsp black pepper. Bring to a gentle boil on medium-high heat, reduce the heat to medium and add fish paste, stirring quickly for 15 seconds, then transfer to a serving bowl.

In a sauce bowl, combine kimchi, the remaining 1 tsp sugar and 1 tsp sesame oil and set aside.

Place noodles in a large microwave-safe serving bowl and heat in a microwave on high for 2 minutes. Bring the soup to a boil on high heat, then pour it over the noodles. Drizzle the remaining 1 tsp sesame oil over the noodles and sprinkle with green onions. Serve with the fried onions, eggs, kimchi, beef and fish paste mixture as condiments.

ASIA IS home to such an abundance of fruit that desserts are often as simple as a plate of sliced mangoes and papayas, or deep-fried bananas. Aside from fruit, Asian desserts can basically be divided into "dry" rolls, buns and pastries and "wet" puddings and sweet soups served at the end of the meal. More recently, thanks to the introduction of ovens and Western recipes, baked cakes and pastries have become more common.

Sweet soups are served as the final course to help with digestion or provide other health benefits, and a Chinese banquet meal always ends with a dry and a wet dessert. In general, though, desserts are purely for indulgence, so go ahead and treat yourself! Deep-Fried Sesame Balls with Red Bean Paste and Golden Kabocha with Walnuts and Honey are bite-size pieces of sweet, crispy and chewy decadence. In contrast, the Custard Dumplings, Green Tea Tiramisu and Mini Ice Wine Moon Cakes fuse North American and Asian flavours and traditions in deeply unusual and delicious sweets. Forget fortune cookies—these are the real Asian desserts!

DESSERTS

"LOVELY LADY" SPECIAL BUBBLE TEA

Makes 3 to 4 cups

2 tsp basil seeds

16 oz watermelon juice

1 Tbsp white sugar

½ cup ice chips

2 oz premade kanten jelly,
in ¼-inch cubes

3 oz seeded watermelon,
in ½-inch cubes

DESSERT DYNASTY introduced bubble tea to Metro Vancouver, and this drink culture subsequently exploded across the city when a massive influx of immigrants from Taiwan, where bubble tea originated, landed in the Lower Mainland. Dessert Dynasty may not be a fancy place, but it still serves the most original bubble teas.

The bubbles in bubble tea are often chewy "pearls" made with tapioca or sago flour. And the "tea" can be any variety or even fruit drinks of any flavour. This recipe uses basil seeds, which are loaded with antioxidants with anti-cancer properties and resemble tiny pearls when soaked, and kanten, which is an agar-agar that's high in fibre but free of fat and cholesterol. Purchase basil seeds and premade kanten in its jelly form in Asian markets, or make your own by bringing 2 cups water to a boil on high and adding 1½ oz kanten powder. Boil uncovered for a couple of minutes, stirring gently, until kanten dissolves and becomes liquid. Pour into a 4-inch square pan, allow to cool for 15 minutes and refrigerate, covered, for 2 to 3 hours until it solidifies to a jelly-like consistency.

IN A MEDIUM saucepan, bring 2 cups water to a gentle boil on high heat. Add basil seeds and immediately turn off the heat. Allow seeds to soak for 5 minutes or until they become translucent. Pour seeds into a colander, drain and rinse under cold running water for 90 seconds. Transfer seeds to an airtight container and refrigerate until needed.

In a blender, combine watermelon juice, sugar and ice chips and blend on high for 60 to 90 seconds. Evenly divide kanten jelly, basil seeds and watermelon cubes among 3 or 4 large, tall glasses. Pour watermelon juice over the jelly and serve ice cold.

DEEP-FRIED SESAME BALLS
with Red Bean Paste

Makes 18 to 20 pieces

3 Tbsp wheat starch	6 cups + 3 Tbsp vegetable oil
4 oz white sugar	½ lb white sesame seeds
1 pkg (400 g) glutinous rice flour	½ lb red bean paste

IN A MEDIUM bowl, combine wheat starch with ½ cup hot water and set aside for 15 minutes. Stir in sugar, rice flour, 3 Tbsp vegetable oil and 1 cup cold water, then knead until the dough binds together.

Line a plate with waxed paper and set aside. Place sesame seeds in a shallow bowl.

Pinch off a 2-Tbsp piece of dough. Place it between your palms and roll it into a 1½-inch ball. Flatten the ball to a ¾-inch-thick round. Place 2 tsp of red bean paste in the middle of the dough. Using your thumb and index finger, fold the edges of the dough towards the middle, covering the red bean paste completely. Gently roll the dough between your palms, shaping it back into a ball without exposing any of the red bean paste. Dip the dough ball in the sesame seeds and roll it around until the surface is evenly coated, then place it on the waxed paper–lined plate. Repeat with the remaining dough and red bean paste.

Line a large plate with paper towels. In a medium saucepan or a deep fryer, heat 6 cups vegetable oil to 350°F. Gently place sesame balls in the oil, being careful not to overcrowd them (fry in batches if necessary), and cook for about 10 minutes or until they float to the top. Cook for another 1 to 2 minutes until golden brown. Using a slotted spoon, transfer the balls to the paper towel–lined plate to drain. Allow to cool for 5 minutes before serving.

SWEETENED BEAN and nut pastes are common filling ingredients for Chinese and Japanese pastries. The combination of glutinous rice flour and wheat starch, a common dough formula for Asian pastries, renders a delicate taffy texture that enhances the dense pastes nicely. Look for them in packages in the flour section of Asian supermarkets or in the bulk food section of some baking supply stores. Packaged pastes, fresh and/or sweetened, are available at Chinese and Japanese supermarkets.

GOLDEN KABOCHA

with Walnuts and Honey

Serves 6 to 8

1 small kabocha squash, about 2 lbs

6 cups vegetable oil, for deep-frying

½ cup all-purpose flour

½ tsp baking soda

2 Tbsp canola oil

1 Tbsp white vinegar

2 Tbsp liquid honey

½ cup whole walnuts

1 tsp roasted white sesame seeds

CUT SQUASH IN half, then peel and discard the skin. Scrape seeds and veins and discard them. Cut squash in ¾- × 2-inch dice.

In a wok or a deep fryer, heat vegetable oil to 375°F. Line a large plate with paper towels.

In a large bowl, whisk together flour, baking soda, canola oil, vinegar and 2 cups cold water to make a smooth batter. Using tongs, dip each piece of squash in the batter, then place it in the oil and deep-fry for 2 to 3 minutes until golden. Place on the paper towel–lined plate to drain.

In a small nonstick pan, heat honey on medium-low. Add walnuts, turning them to ensure they are coated evenly with honey.

Divide kabocha among 6 to 8 plates, drizzle with honey and walnuts and sprinkle with sesame seeds. Serve hot.

CHEF CHAN'S tempura-inspired creation steps away from the sweet soups and paste-stuffed pastries traditionally associated with Asian desserts and turns the focus on the naturally sweet, tender and wholesome kabocha winter squash. In this recipe, the squash is lightly battered, quickly dipped in oil and drizzled with honey to create morsels that are crispy on the outside with a slightly starchy interior. This dish received not only the Best Dessert honour at the 2009 Vancouver Chinese Restaurant Awards but also thumbs-up reviews in *Condé Nast Traveler* and other publications.

GREEN TEA TIRAMISU

Makes a 9- × 13-inch cake

18 oz mascarpone cheese, room temperature

5 eggs, separated

3 Tbsp green tea powder

1 Tbsp powdered gelatin

½ cup + 7 Tbsp white sugar

40 ladyfinger biscuits, each 4 inches

ZEST IS a casual fine-dining restaurant serving classic Japanese dishes presented in a non-traditional modern dining room. It's especially well known for its wine pairings and its desserts of the day, including this tiramisu.

Thick and easily spreadable triple-cream mascarpone cheese, made with fresh cream, is the classic ingredient for Italian tiramisu. Green tea powder is the extracted powder form of green tea, the finest being Japanese matcha, which is made with superior-quality green tea and used in traditional tea ceremonies. Begin this dessert at least a day before you plan to serve it so that it has time to set overnight.

PLACE MASCARPONE IN the bowl of a large stand mixer or in a large bowl. Using a fork, add yolks one at a time, turning on the mixer (or a hand-held mixer) for 5 seconds every time a yolk is added. When all yolks are in, blend until well combined. Add 1 Tbsp of the green tea powder, and blend continuously for 4 to 6 minutes until the mixture becomes soft and creamy.

In a large bowl, mix gelatin and 2 Tbsp hot water, stirring for about 1 minute or until powder dissolves. Whip in 1 Tbsp of the green tea powder, 4 cups hot water and 7 Tbsp sugar, and continue to whip for another 2 to 3 minutes until ingredients are well combined.

To make meringue, place egg whites and ½ cup sugar in a medium bowl. Using a hand-held electric mixer, mix on medium-high speed for 5 to 6 minutes or until the mixture becomes foamy and forms soft peaks. Cover and refrigerate until needed.

In a small saucepan, combine 1 Tbsp of the mascarpone mixture and 1 Tbsp of the gelatin mixture. Heat on low for 2 to 3 minutes until mascarpone dissolves completely and the mixture becomes smooth, then slowly pour into the remaining mascarpone mixture and blend for 6 to 8 minutes. Using a spatula, fold in meringue, blending gently for 5 to 8 minutes or until foamy and creamy.

Have ready a 9- × 13-inch glass dish. Quickly soak ladyfingers, 2 or 3 at a time, in the gelatin mixture and place them in a single layer on the bottom of the dish. Spread one-third of the mascarpone mixture evenly over the ladyfingers. Repeat with a second layer of ladyfingers and a second layer of mascarpone. Finish with a final layer of ladyfingers and a final layer of mascarpone. Cover with plastic wrap and refrigerate overnight to set.

Just before serving, sprinkle the remaining 1 Tbsp green tea powder through a fine-mesh sieve to evenly dust the top of the tiramisu. Slice into individual portions and serve slightly chilled.

CUSTARD DUMPLINGS

Makes 20 to 24 dumplings

4 Tbsp butter	2 Tbsp + 1 tsp custard powder	1 cup wheat starch
1 large egg	½ tsp vanilla extract	9 Tbsp glutinous rice flour
4 Tbsp all-purpose flour	4 Tbsp white sugar	2 Tbsp cornstarch

THIS EUROPEAN-INFLUENCED custard filling will remind coconut bun lovers of the intricate texture of that dish's sugary filling. The custard in this recipe needs to be refrigerated for 2 hours before it's used to stuff the dumplings. However, you can prepare this dish ahead of time: stuffed but uncooked dumplings can be frozen in an airtight container for up to 7 days. Serve this dish as a dessert as Northern Delicacy does, or eat it as a snack if you prefer.

IN A FOOD processor, blend butter, egg, all-purpose flour, 2 Tbsp custard powder, vanilla and sugar on high for 2 to 3 minutes, or until the mixture becomes a yolky paste. Transfer to an airtight container and refrigerate for 2 hours. This is the custard filling.

In a large bowl, combine wheat and rice flours, cornstarch and the 1 tsp custard powder until well mixed. Slowly add 1 cup boiling water and, using a whisk, mix until all ingredients are combined. Allow to cool for 15 to 20 minutes. Knead dough for about 10 minutes until smooth. Divide the dough in half and roll into 2 balls, covering them with a damp tea towel so that the dough does not dry out.

Place ¼ cup cold water in a small bowl. Lightly dust a clean work surface with flour. Place one ball of dough on the work surface and, using a rolling pin, roll to a thickness of 1⁄16 inch. With a 3-inch round dough cutter (or an inverted glass), cut 10 to 12 circles.

Lightly dust a baking sheet with flour. One at a time, place a round of dough in front of you and mound 1 Tbsp custard filling in the centre. Dip your index finger in the bowl of cold water, then run it around the edge of the dough to moisten. Fold the bottom half of the dough over the filling to make a half-moon shape. Press the edges together gently to seal them. Transfer the filled dumpling to the baking sheet and cover with a clean tea towel. Repeat with the remaining dough rounds and filling, then roll out the second ball of dough, cut 10 to 12 more rounds and fill them with custard.

Bring 3 cups water to a boil in a 12-inch wok or a saucepan on high heat.

Line a 10-inch bamboo steamer with an 8-inch round waxed-paper doily. (Alternatively, just line the bamboo steamer with a sheet of parchment paper.). Place dumplings on the doily with ½ inch space between them—you should be able to fit on 6 to 8 dumplings. Place the bamboo steamer in the wok (or pot), cover and steam for 10 to 12 minutes, or until dumplings are cooked through. (The dumplings are ready when a knife inserted in the dough comes out easily and the dough becomes creamy yellow.) Remove the steamer from the heat and allow dumplings to cool for 3 to 5 minutes. Repeat, using a new doily each time, until all dumplings are steamed. Serve hot.

MINI ICE WINE MOON CAKES

Makes 25 to 30 mini moon cakes

MOON CAKE CRUST	½ cup + 1 Tbsp vegetable oil
½ cup + 1 Tbsp maple syrup	2 cups pastry flour + extra for dusting
6 Tbsp honey	1 egg

MID-AUTUMN FESTIVAL, also known as the Moon Festival, is an annual harvest celebration that takes place wherever Chinese people gather on August 15th of the lunar calendar, when the moon is at its fullest. Round moon cakes, stuffed with sweet paste (made from nuts, seeds and beans), egg yolks and other goodies, are the most cherished food during the Moon Festival. They are traditionally given to friends and family members as a token of friendship.

This recipe makes moon cakes with a chewy crust typical of the Cantonese style. In Taiwan and Shanghai the crust is usually flakier, like a puff pastry. In certain Chinese provinces, moon cakes are simply any sweet stuffed pastry. Prepare the dough the night before you plan to make the cakes. And use a wooden moon cake mould, available from Asian cook shops, to make the cakes. Munch on the cakes at any time of day.

Chef Daryl Nagata, executive chef at the Pan Pacific Hotel, often combines Asian and West Coast flavours and techniques, but this moon cake developed with pastry shef Hans Pirhofer is a truly original signature dish whose filling pairs traditional lotus seed paste with ice wine, hazelnuts and other Canadian ingredients. Available only to guests who attend the Pan Pacific Hotel's Moon Festival brunch, a sold-out annual event that features exquisite B.C. and Asian dishes, these treats are the perfect ending to a special occasion dinner.

MOON CAKE CRUST In a medium bowl, combine maple syrup, honey, vegetable oil and ½ Tbsp water and mix well. Place flour in a large bowl and, using a fork, slowly stir in the syrup mixture until just mixed, 2 to 3 minutes. Do not overmix, or the dough will become dry. Cover with plastic wrap and refrigerate overnight.

ICE WINE FILLING In a medium bowl, combine lotus seed paste, hazelnuts, walnuts, dried fruit and ice wine until well mixed.

FINISH CAKES Lightly dust a clean work surface with flour. Unwrap dough and, using a rolling pin, roll into a 10-inch square about ⅛ inch thick. Using a 4-inch round cookie cutter or a small ramekin, cut dough into discs.

Preheat the oven to 400°F. Lightly grease a large baking sheet.

Lightly dust mould(s) with flour. Place a disc of dough on a cake mould, making sure it is evenly aligned. Gently press the dough into the mould to fill all cracks, leaving the excess dough hanging over the side of the mould. Spoon 1½ Tbsp of the filling into the mould, pressing it down gently to fill any air pockets. Fold the dough over the filling to completely encase it, then press the edges together and smooth them by hand to seal the cake. Invert the mould onto the counter, tapping it until the cake comes loose. Place cake on the baking sheet, leaving at least ½ inch space around it. Repeat with the remaining dough and filling. You should have 25 to 30 mini cakes.

ICE WINE FILLING

1¼ cups lotus seed paste, room temperature

¼ cup hazelnuts, crushed

¼ cup walnuts, crushed

¼ cup dried berries of your choice

¼ cup Canadian ice wine

In a bowl, whisk egg with a pinch of salt until foamy. Brush half of the egg wash evenly over moon cakes. Bake on the middle rack for 15 minutes. Brush cakes with the remaining egg wash and bake for 15 to 20 minutes more, or until golden brown. Remove from the oven and allow to cool. Serve warm or at room temperature.

Moon cake mould

GOLDEN VILLAGE / RICHMOND

RICHMOND IS KNOWN as Little Asia or the New Chinatown because 43.6 per cent of its population, the largest number in any Canadian municipality in 2006, is of Chinese descent. Its Golden Village, the area along No. 3 Road that has a concentration of Asian malls, markets and restaurants, is now easily reached by SkyTrain from downtown Vancouver. From Richmond Centre and Lansdowne Centre to Yaohan Centre, Empire Centre and the enormous Aberdeen Centre, each shopping mall is packed with Asian-themed stores, grocery stores and dim sum houses and ethnic restaurants, each with its own character and attractions that take hours to explore. Here's where you can browse fashion stores and trendy shops alongside gaggles of young Asians, sit down for a meal beside three generations of the same family and listen to a conversation carried out in Cantonese, Mandarin and English.

For some of the best mall eats in the Golden Village, visit Aberdeen Centre, whose food court contains such well-known fare as Beard Papa's cream puffs, Café D'Lite's laksa noodles and Jang Mo Jib's Korean barbecue dishes (then stroll through Daiso, the two-dollar megastore). The mall is also home to such award-winning restaurants as Tropika (Thai and Malaysian), Northern Delicacy (Shanghai and Sichuanese) and Fisherman's Terrace (dim sum and seafood).

A 10-minute walk from Aberdeen Centre is Richmond's restaurant strip, Alexandra Road, where deciding which restaurant to dine in will likely take more than 10 minutes. (This street is called *wai sek kai*, "Eating Street," by locals.) The options range from a medley of Chinese dim sum and seafood houses, including the award-winning Jade Seafood Restaurant and Empire Chinese Cuisine, to Japanese sushi places and izakayas, Korean barbecue houses, Taiwanese cafés, Chinese noodle and you-cook hot pot places. Since eating out is a popular pastime for Asian families, reservations are highly recommended for Friday dinners, and for both lunch and dinner on Saturdays and Sundays!

Not on Alexandra Road but still close by are Delicious Cuisine and Zephyr Tea House Café, beautifully decorated Taiwanese cafés that sit side by side on the other side of No. 3 Road off Alderbridge Way. Other great bets in Richmond include Bubble Fruity on Saba Road, which specializes in Chinese dessert soups; the Shanghainese Suhang Restaurant, especially for beggar's chicken (mud-baked chicken Hangzhou-style) stuffed with sticky rice, wrapped in lotus leaves and then cooked in a mud ball, which is as interesting to look at as it is tasty; and New Asia Deli and Pearl Castle, two of the dozens of Asian eateries inside Continental Centre, a strip mall on Sexsmith Road.

Richmond is also home to the largest Asian-style open market outside of Asia, the Summer Night Market along River Road that operates from May to September. Located in a large field by the river in an industrial zone and filled with hundreds of red awnings, the market offers electronic and household products, pet supplies and trendy fashions as well as centre-stage entertainment and contests (including eating and food-related challenges). The most talked-about feature is the huge, smoky street food area serving global fare such as Cantonese fish balls, dragon beard thread desserts, Korean pancakes, roasted corn, Filipino barbecue, Vietnamese spring rolls, dim sum, Japanese takoyaki, roti, bubble teas and Taiwanese desserts. Squeeze through the crowds to peer into the sizzling woks, hissing steamers and bubbling deep fryers. Although plastic forks and flimsy chopsticks are provided if you want to sample, go ahead and use your fingers. Everyone is welcome, and admission is free!

Asian cleaver A big, heavy-set knife with a rectangular blade used in Asian kitchens. Heavier cleavers with longer, wider blades are usually used for chopping and cutting thick meats, while lighter cleavers with thinner blades are used for slicing and cutting vegetables.

Asian spatula A short stainless steel or carbon steel version of a shovel with a round edge designed for stir-frying and tossing large quantities of heavy food.

Bamboo or wood skewers Long, thin bamboo or wooden sticks used for grilling food over direct heat. Soak the sticks in water so that they are thoroughly wet before you use them, to prevent burning. Japanese also use skewers to check the readiness of food while it's cooking without blemishing it.

Bamboo steamers Round, flat-bottomed woven bamboo containers of different sizes that, when set over a pot or wok of boiling water, allow hot air to stream upward and steam-cook the contents within. The usual sizes range from 4 to 12 inches in diameter, and a matching cover should come as part of the set. Clean the steamers with a mild detergent and a soft cloth, rinse them under warm running water and blot dry with a towel. Air-dry the steamers away from the sun.

Ceramic pot (Clay pot, Sand pot) A round clay or ceramic pot available in a variety of sizes for cooking rice, stews and hot pot entrées. Buy one with two handles for safer, easier handling.

Chinese fondue pot A 10- to 14-inch round steel pot with a divider down the middle that creates two even compartments so that two different soup stocks can be used at the same time. A good fondue pot should have heatproof handles and a flat bottom so that it can sit securely on a portable butane stove set on the table. It comes in a carrying case for convenient storage.

Chinese fondue skimmers Small wire baskets with long handles, used to cook ingredients in a Chinese fondue pot. Each guest at a fondue meal receives a skimmer and a set of chopsticks.

Chopsticks (Hashi) Originally made from branches of even length, chopsticks are now shaped from polished processed wood, plastic or often bamboo, too. In Korea, most chopsticks are made of stainless steel. A pair of chopsticks is still an essential eating implement in much of Asia.

Daikon grater A flat-bottomed bowl-shaped container with a raised surface full of holes used for grating daikon and ginger, this is an essential tool for Japanese cookery, as it grates finely while capturing all the juice. The steel grater looks like a regular cheese grater but has a longer handle. Substitute a box grater set in a bowl, if you don't have a daikon grater.

Hangiri Used for mixing steamed rice with seasoned vinegar to make sushi rice, this large, round wooden bowl or tub cools and aerates the grains. Varying in size from 15 inches to 28 inches and usually made of cypress wood, the large surface releases steam and cools the rice evenly as you mix. Although the cypress wood imparts a distinct flavour to the rice, you can use a wooden salad bowl as a substitute, if necessary.

Makisu A bamboo mat for making and rolling sushi. Most mats are 10 inches square, but the size does vary. Look for well-lined and securely fastened mats and clean them with mild detergent and a soft cloth under warm running water. Air-dry the mats away from the sun.

Mortar and pestle Instead of a blender or food processor, this is the tool recommended for grinding fresh or dried herbs and spices. Look for hard, solid mortars with a deep-set bowl made of stone or wood. The pestle should be a thick cylinder with round edges and made of the same material as the mortar.

Noodle strainer A large wire, cup-sized strainer with a long wooden heatproof handle to remove cooked noodles from boiling water. The cup helps to measure the quantity of noodles and holds them in place during the boiling process.

Otoshi buta (Drop lid) A flat wooden lid floated directly on simmering liquids in a pot. It is used in Japanese cooking to gently hold delicate foods in place so that they do not lose their original shape and to distribute heat more evenly.

Portable butane stove A tabletop single-burner stove fuelled by disposable butane canisters for Asian hot pot (fondue-style) meals. Both the stove and canister (sold separately) come in a single size and are available at Asian supermarkets and kitchen stores.

Rice cooker A must-have gadget in most Asian households, an electric rice cooker is the easiest way to cook rice of any kind. For cooking rice, buy a simple model instead of a multi-purpose one.

Shamoji A flat wooden, round-headed spoon or paddle designed with soft edges that won't cut the rice grains and used mostly to fold and serve rice in Japanese and Chinese kitchens.

Sushi or sashimi knife The most important utensil in the sushi chef's kitchen. A clean and razor-sharp knife is the key to perfect cuts of meat and fish, and chefs are fastidious about maintaining their knives before, during and after cooking by cleaning and wiping the blade with a soft cloth after every few cuts and sharpening the blade on a whetstone every day. Made of stainless steel, a sashimi knife has a long, narrow shield-like blade with a pointed tip and ranges from 1 to 10 inches long. A wooden handle with a good grip allows the chef to cut with precision.

Wok The must-have utensil for Asian cookery, a wok is used for boiling water, making soup, cooking rice, steaming, stir-frying and deep-frying. The original woks were made from iron, then carbon steel, stainless steel or aluminum. Nowadays, even Teflon is used but cast iron or carbon steel best retain their shape and distribute heat evenly. Look for a wok that's at least 3 inches deep and has a round bottom, which will evenly distribute the heat. Use a wok stand if you have electric elements or a flat stove surface. It should come with a matching lid but, if not, buy one on the spot to ensure it's the right size and height. A 14-inch wok is the most common size, but 10 inches in diameter or larger is functional for basic stir-frying or pan-frying.

To treat a new carbon steel or stainless steel wok, soak in hot water with a few drops of liquid detergent, then clean and dry it with a sponge. Season it before cooking by setting it on medium heat and rubbing it evenly with a lump of raw pork fat, then wiping it dry with a paper towel. Repeat this seasoning process a few times until the paper towel shows no traces of black residue. Like cast-iron pans, woks should never be washed with soap or harsh detergents.

Wok brush A basic brush is made of thin strips of bamboo or wood gathered in a cluster and wound with twine at one end. A fancier version has a wooden or bamboo handle inset with long bristles. Still used in many Asian restaurant kitchens, it's used to brush the wok under very hot running water to remove any residue without using detergent.

Wok ring A large, rigid stainless steel or carbon steel circle used to stabilize the wok on flat surfaces. It can be placed on a countertop or over a stovetop burner.

Wok steamer A wire ring or perforated stainless steel rack that can be placed inside a wok to hold a bamboo steamer or food for steaming.

Asian

Asian Way Supermarket
2800 East 1st Avenue, Vancouver.
604-251-3006

Banana Grove Market and Deli
2705 East 22nd Avenue,
Vancouver. 604-435-0646

Dong Thanh Supermarket
1172 Kingsway, Vancouver.
604-873-8534

East West Market
4169 Main Street, Vancouver.
604-873-8082

Grand Value Asian Market
20–8251 Westminster Highway,
Richmond. 604-273-9877

Grand Western Asian Market
4096 Oxford Street, Burnaby.
604-298-9515

Granville Island Public Market
www.granvilleisland.com
1689 Johnston Street, Vancouver.
604-666-5784

Osaka Supermarket
3700 No. 3 Road, Richmond.
604-276-8808

2200 Park Royal South, West
Vancouver. 778-279-8988

South China Seas Trading Co.
www.southchinaseas.ca
125–1689 Johnston Street,
Vancouver. 604-681-5402

1502 Victoria Drive, Vancouver.
604-254-5403

T&T Supermarket
www.tnt-supermarket.com

179 Keefer Place, Vancouver.
604-899-8836

100–2800 East 1st Avenue,
Vancouver. 604-254-9668

1000–8181 Cambie Road,
Richmond. 604-279-1818

15277 100th Avenue, Surrey.
604-930-2388

2740–2929 Barnet Highway,
Coquitlam. 604-945-3818

10153 King George Boulevard,
Surrey. 604-580-3168

147–4800 Kingsway, Burnaby.
604-436-4881

Chinese and Taiwanese

Chinatown Supermarket
239 Keefer Street, Vancouver.
604-685-3583

Cho Farm Market
4151 Hazelbridge Way, Richmond.
604-233-1968

Chong Lee Market
3308 East 22nd Avenue,
Vancouver. 604-432-6880

6399 Victoria Drive, Vancouver.
604-323-8133

1772 Renfrew Street, Vancouver.
604-677-0026

Good Neighbour Crystal Mall
Supermarket
4500 Kingsway, Burnaby.
604-438-7216

Great One Supermarket
8131 Park Road, Richmond.
604-279-8928

Hing Shing Market
1757 Kingsway Vancouver.
604-873-4938

Joyce 99 Market
3369 Kingsway, Vancouver.
604-438-1195

Lian Hua Grocery Store
4500 Kingsway, Burnaby.
604-568-3360

New Hong Kong Supermarket
1178–3779 Sexsmith Road,
Richmond. 604-231-0810

Oriental Food Mart
1292 Kingsway, Vancouver.
604-873-3727

South Burnaby Market
7890 6th Street, Burnaby.
604-516-8666

Star Asian Food Centre
2053 West 41st Avenue,
Vancouver. 604-263-2892

Sunrise Markets
300 Powell Street, Vancouver.
604-685-8019

Super 8
4500 Kingsway, Burnaby.
604-433-1777

Tin Cheung Market
6414 Victoria Drive, Vancouver.
604-322-9237

Two Thousand Supermarket
1418–8388 Capstan Way,
Richmond. 604-232-1318

Wah Shang Supermarket
8108 Park Road, Richmond.
604-278-8309

234–2800 East 1st Avenue,
Vancouver. 604-251-2799

Western Rice Mills
www.westernricemills.com
6231 Westminster Highway,
Richmond. 604-284-5162

Filipino

71 Food Store
8710 Granville Street, Vancouver.
604-263-6018

Aling Mary's
8085 Park Road, Richmond.
604-231-1918

2656 Main Street, Vancouver.
604-873-6005

13979 104th Avenue, Surrey.
604-930-6059

Aling Pining
4245 Fraser Street, Vancouver.
604-873-0519

Bayanihan Pinoy Food Mart
12153 Harris Road, Pitt Meadows.
604-465-0048

Fiesta Filipino Grocery
222 Lonsdale Avenue, North
Vancouver. 604-983-9111

114 West 15th Avenue, North
Vancouver. 604-983-0301

Jeepney Mart
c-1071 Austin Avenue, Coquitlam.
604-936-2745

3229 Kingsway, Vancouver.
604-431-0247

Kababayan Grocery Store
106 East 3rd Street, North
Vancouver. 604-983-0277

Kay Market
5169 Joyce Street, Vancouver.
604-454-9097

Ken Koy Filipino Food
13551 105A Avenue, Surrey.
604-588-4538

Nipa Hut
10059 136A Street, Surrey.
604-957-2842

Pinoy Dragon Mart
919 12th Street, New
Westminster. 604-525-3377

Pinoy Q Mart
6526 Victoria Drive, Vancouver.
604-325-1001

Tatak Pinoy
5032 Joyce Street, Vancouver.
604-568-1009

Tindahan Grocery
120–5960 Minoru Boulevard,
Richmond. 604-304-0469

Indian and Punjabi

All India Foods
6517 Main Street, Vancouver.
604-324-2195

Fruiticana
www.fruiticana.com

6387 Fraser Street, Vancouver.
604-321-9931

4101 No. 5 Road, Richmond.
604-244-9520

15933 Fraser Highway, Surrey.
604-593-5163

12788 76A Avenue, Surrey.
604-597-1676

12047 80th Avenue, Surrey.
604-591-5032

18438 64th Avenue, Cloverdale.
778-597-0999

13787 72nd Avenue, Surrey.
604-590-2080

13639 100th Avenue, Surrey.
604-585-6100

2807 Shaughnessy Street, Port
Coquitlam. 604-464-0822

31205 MacLure Road,
Abbotsford. 604-504-5877

13174 64th Street, Surrey.
604-598-9220

7028 120th Street Surrey.
604-590-8864

12855 96th Street, Surrey.
604-588-6620

JB Foods
6607 Main Street, Vancouver.
604-321-0224

Patel's Specialty and
Bulk Food Store
2210 Commercial Drive,
Vancouver. 604-255-6729

Polo Market
6475 Fraser Street, Vancouver.
604-321-7117

Punjabi Food Centre
6635 Main Street, Vancouver.
604-322-5502

Sidhu's Supermarket
7565 6th Street, Burnaby.
604-540-6032

Spicy Land
9336 120 Street, Surrey.
604-951-0566

Japanese

Datong Japanese Food Store
4500 Kingsway, Burnaby.
604-436-0499

Fujiya Foods
www.fujiya.ca

912 Clark Drive, Vancouver.
604-251-3711

113–3086 St. Edwards Drive,
Richmond. 604-270-3715

112–1050 West Pender Street,
Vancouver. 604-608-1050

624 Shelbourne Street, Victoria.
250-598-3711

Izumi-Ya Japanese Market Place
7971 Alderbridge Way, Richmond.
604-303-1171

Konbiniya Japanese Centre
1238 Robson Street, Vancouver.
604-682-3634

Minato Food Market
3900 Steveston Highway,
Richmond. 604-271-7732

Korean

Han Nam Supermarket
www.hannamsm.com

4501 North Road, Burnaby.
604-420-8856

1–15357 104th Avenue, Surrey.
604-580-3433

H-Mart (Han Ah Reum Mart)
590 Robson Street, Vancouver.
604-609-4567

329 North Road, Coquitlam.
604-939-0135

19555 Fraser Highway, Surrey.
604-539-1377

Hyundai Oriental Food Market
3488 Kingsway, Vancouver.
604-874-1651

Kim's Mart
519 West Broadway, Vancouver.
604-872-8885

Thai and Vietnamese

88 Supermarket
4801 Victoria Drive, Vancouver.
604-876-2128

Binh Duong Grocery Store
717 East Broadway, Vancouver.
604-873-4845

Can Tho Market
3345 Fraser Street, Vancouver.
604-876-4551

Hen Long Market
14357 104th Avenue, Surrey.
604-585-8588

My Tho Supermarket
1106 Kingsway, Vancouver.
604-879-2718

Sieu Thi Wong Xin Market
747 Gore Avenue, Vancouver.
604-688-8235

Thuan Phat Supermarket
377 East Broadway, Vancouver.
604-873-8587

Viet Hoa Market
724 Kingsway, Vancouver.
604-876-6350

Western Oriental Market
101–1050 Kingsway, Vancouver.
604-876-4711

Wing Sang Meat and
Vegetable Market
3755 Main Street, Vancouver.
604-879-6866

Others

Galloway's Specialty Foods
www.gallowaysfoods.com

110–8620 Glenlyon Parkway,
Burnaby. 604-430-6363

7860 Alderbridge Way,
Richmond. 604-270-6363

Featured Restaurants

Alvin Garden
4850 Imperial Street, Burnaby.
604-437-0828

Always Seafood Restaurant
4298 Main Street, Vancouver.
604-876-6110

Ashiana Tandoori
www.ashianatandoori.com

1440 Kingsway, Vancouver.
604-874-5060

200–8072 120 Street, Surrey.
604-593-5458

Bao Bei Chinese Brasserie
www.bao-bei.ca
163 Keefer Street, Vancouver.
604-688-0876

Blue Water Cafe + Raw Bar
www.bluewatercafe.net
1095 Hamilton Street, Vancouver.
604-688-8078

Bon Café
4909 Main Street, Vancouver.
604-325-1199

Buk Jang Do Ga Korean Cuisine
19539 Fraser Highway, Surrey.
778-278-0788

Cactus Club Cafe
www.cactusclubcafe.com

1136 Robson Street, Vancouver.
604-687-3278

588 Burrard Street, Vancouver.
604-682-0933

1530 West Broadway, Vancouver.
604-733-0434

575 West Broadway, Vancouver.
604-714-6000

357 Davie Street, Vancouver.
604-685-8070

7320 Market Crossing, Burnaby.
604-430-5000

4219B Lougheed Highway,
Burnaby. 604-291-6606

4653 Kingsway, Burnaby.
604-431-8448

111–101 Schoolhouse Street,
Coquitlam. 604-777-0440

855 Main Street, West Vancouver.
604-922-1707

900 Main Street, West Vancouver.
604-922-8882

1598 Pemberton Avenue, North
Vancouver. 604-986-5776

5500 No. 3 Road, Richmond.
604-244-9969

15079 32nd Avenue, Surrey.
604-535-8799

Café D'Lite
www.cafedlite.com
3144 West Broadway, Vancouver.
604-733-8882

Café Kathmandu
www.cafekathmandu.com
2779 Commercial Drive,
Vancouver. 604-879-9909

Celadon Fine Korean Cuisine
300–4293 Mountain Square,
Whistler. 604-905-4188

Charm Modern Thai
www.charmmodernthai.com
1269 Hamilton Street, Vancouver.
604-688-9339

Chinese Bistro
thechinesebistro.tumblr.com
4274 Mountain Square, Whistler.
604-962-0328

Chutney Villa
www.chutneyvilla.com
147 East Broadway, Vancouver.
604-872-2228

Coast Plaza Hotel and Suites
1763 Comox Street, Vancouver.
604-688-7711

Cru Restaurant
www.cru.ca
1459 West Broadway, Vancouver.
604-677-4111

Curry 2 U
www.curry2you.com
281–1689 Johnston Street,
Granville Island Public Market,
Vancouver. 604-662-7778

Delicious Cuisine
7911 Alderbridge Way, Richmond.
604-207-1388

Dessert Dynasty
www.dessertdynasty.com
149–4800 Kingsway, Metropolis
@ Metrotown, Burnaby.
604-438-8608

Dirty Apron Cooking School
www.dirtyapron.com
540 Beatty Street, Vancouver.
604-879-8588

Edible Canada at the Market
www.ediblecanada.com
/bistro.php
1596 Johnston Street, Granville
Island Public Market, Vancouver.
604-682-6681

Evergreen Vegetarian House
1155–4540 No. 3 Road,
Richmond. 604-879-3380

Fiesta Filipino Restaurant
222 Lonsdale Avenue, North
Vancouver. 604-983-9111

Hapa Izakaya
www.hapaizakaya.com

1479 Robson Street, Vancouver.
604-689-4272

1516 Yew Street, Vancouver.
604-738-4272

1193 Hamilton Street, Vancouver.
604-681-4272

Hon's Wun-Tun House
www.hons.ca

268 Keefer Street, Vancouver.
604-688-0871

1339 Robson Street, Vancouver.
604-685-0871

310–3025 Lougheed Highway,
Coquitlam. 604-468-0871

408–6th Street, New
Westminster. 604-520-6661

iCafé Restaurant
www.icafe-restaurant.com
2525 Heather Street, Vancouver.
604-630-0238

Jade Dynasty Restaurant
137 East Pender Street,
Vancouver. 604-683-8816

James Snacks
4540 No. 3 Road, Richmond.
604-716-1328

Ken's Chinese Restaurant
www.kenschineserestaurant.com
1097 Kingsway, Vancouver.
604-873-6338

Kirin Restaurant
www.kirinrestaurants.com

1172 Alberni Street, Vancouver.
604-682-8833

201 City Square, 555 West
12th Avenue, Vancouver.
604-879-8038

200 Three West Centre,
7900 Westminster Highway,
Richmond. 604-303-8833

2001 Henderson Place,
1163 Pinetree Way, Coquitlam.
604-944-8833

350 Gifford Street, New
Westminster. 604-528-8833

Lin Chinese Cuisine
and Tea House
www.linchinese.ca
1537 West Broadway, Vancouver.
604-733-9696

Long's Noodle House
4853 Main Street, Vancouver.
604-879-7879

Maenam
www.maenam.ca
1938 West 4th Avenue, Vancouver.
604-730-5579

Master Hung BBQ Restaurant
8780 Blundell Road, Richmond.
604-272-3813

New Asia Deli
1113–3779 Sexsmith Road,
Richmond. 604-279-4288

Northern Delicacy
www.northern-delicacy.com
2788–4151 Hazelbridge Way,
Aberdeen Centre, Richmond.
604-233-7050

Pacific Institute of Culinary Arts
www.picachef.com
1505 West 2nd Avenue,
Vancouver. 604-734-4488

Pan Pacific Hotel Vancouver
www.panpacificvancouver.com
300–999 Canada Place,
Vancouver. 604-662-8111

SalaThai Thai Restaurant
www.salathai.ca
102–888 Burrard Street,
Vancouver. 604-683-7999

Shaktea
www.shaktea.ca
3702 Main Street, Vancouver.
604-873-5151

ShuRaku Sake Bar and Bistro
www.shuraku.net
833 Granville Street, Vancouver.
604-687-6622

Spice Islands Indonesian
Restaurant
www.spiceislandsindonesian.com
3592 West 41st Avenue,
Vancouver. 604-266-7355

Spring Garden Chinese Seafood
Restaurant
832 12th Street, New
Westminster. 604-525-6000

Sun Fresh Bakery
245 Keefer Street, Vancouver.
604-688-3868

Sun Sui Wah Seafood Restaurant
www.sunsuiwah.com

3888 Main Street, Vancouver.
604-872-8822

102–4940 No. 3 Road, Richmond.
604-273-8208

Tamarind Hill Malaysian Cuisine
www.tamarindhill.ca

103–628 6th Avenue, New
Westminster. 604-526-3000

1440 Lonsdale Avenue, North
Vancouver. 604-990-0111

Terracotta Modern Chinese
www.terracottavancouver.com
52 Alexander Street, Vancouver.
604-569-3088

Thai House
www.thaihouse.com/
thai-house-restaurant

1116 Robson Street, Vancouver.
604-683-3383

1766 West 7th Avenue, Vancouver.
604-737-0088

116 West Esplanade, North
Vancouver. 604-987-9911

129–4940 No. 3 Road, Richmond.
604-278-7373

Thai in the Village
www.thaiinthevillage.com
300–4293 Mountain Square,
Whistler. 604-935-8828

**Tina Fineza Service Excellence
Restaurant Consultants**
tinafineza@hotmail.com
Vancouver. 604-551-7755

Tojo's
www.tojos.com
1133 West Broadway, Vancouver.
604-872-8050

Tropika
www.tropika-canada.com

1128 Robson Street, Vancouver.
604-737-6002

2975 Cambie Street, Vancouver.
604-879-6002

1830–4151 Hazelbridge Way,
Aberdeen Centre, Richmond.
604-233-7002

West Restaurant
www.westrestaurant.com
2881 Granville Street, Vancouver.
604-738-8938

Westview Oriental Restaurant
www.westviewchinese.com
108–2609 Westview Drive, North
Vancouver. 604-987-7799

Wild Rice
www.wildricevancouver.com
117 West Pender Street,
Vancouver. 604-642-2882

Zephyr Tea House Café
100A–7911 Alderbridge Way,
Richmond. 604-270-2588

Zest Japanese Cuisine
www.zestjapanese.com
2775 West 16th Avenue,
Vancouver. 604-731-9378

INDEX

BOLD page numbers indicate definitions; *italics* indicate photos.

Japanese horseradish.
    See wasabi
Japanese salsa verde with
    salmon tempura and
    avocado strips, 94–95, *95*
jellyfish and chicken salad, 63
jiang. *See* ginger
jiang yu. *See* soy sauce
jicama, **19**
ji chai, **19**
jit gua. *See* hairy melon

kabocha with walnuts
    and honey, *188*, 189
kaffir limes, **19**
kanten. *See* Japanese gelatin
kaofu, **28**
kaofu with mushrooms,
    wood ears and bamboo
    shoots, 166–67, *167*
kasu and chili bean sauce with
    salmon steaks, 111
kebabs, spicy chicken, 120, *121*
kecap manis, **28**. *See also* sambal
KIMCHI (KIMCHEE), **28**
    casserole soup, 50
    and noodles in dried
        anchovy broth, 182–83
king onions. *See* Chinese onions
kinome, **9**
kombu (konbu), **29**
Korean-style BBQ pork
    lettuce wraps, 74–75, *75*
kun choy. *See* Chinese celery

laab gai (Thai minced
    chicken salad), 64
LAMB
    chops, lemon grass, 140–41
    chops, marinated, 140–41
    chops, minted, 142
    jalfrezi, 143
laos. *See* galangal
lap chong. *See* Chinese sausages
lap yok. *See* Chinese bacon
larb beef, 134, *135*
lau Thai (spicy Vietnamese
    seafood hot pot), *113*, 114–15
LEMON GRASS, **10**, *127*
    with grilled chicken, 127

lamb chops, 140–41
    marinade, 140
lentils, **20**. *See also* dal, mung beans
lettuce wraps, BBQ pork, 74–75, *75*
lily buds, dried, **17**, *17*
limes, kaffir, **19**
lingcod in a ponzu and
    dashi broth with
    Shanghai bok choy, 110
lo bok. *See* daikon
LOTUS
    leaves, **20**
    root, **20**, *59*
    root, in twenty-first
        century salad, 58–59
    seed paste, in ice wine
        filling, 194–195
    seeds, **20**
"lovely lady" special
    bubble tea, 186

mace, **10**
Malaysian spicy pan mee
    noodles, 176–77, *177*
mango pepper potatoes, 165
mango powder, **10**
marinated lamb chops, 140–41
marinated spinach salad
    (gomae), 57
matsutake, **20**
meat. *See* chicken; beef; duck;
    goat; lamb; pork
mei gui lu cooking wine, **29**
MELON
    bitter, **14**, *14*
    and Dungeness
        crab soup, 44, *45*
    hairy, **19**
    winter, **24**
    in yin-yang salad, 61
milk fritters, crispy, 104
minced chicken salad, 64
mini ice wine moon cakes, 194–95
mint, **10**
minted lamb chops, 142
mirin, **29**
miso, **29**
mitsuba, **10**, *10*
mizuna, **20**
mo gua. *See* hairy melon

moon cakes, ice wine, 194–95
mung bean pancakes, 87
mung beans, **21**.
    See also dal; lentils
MUSHROOM(S). *See also* fungus
    and bean curd, carrot
        and celery wraps, 82–83
    and bean sprouts on
        vermicelli, 173
    and chicken in a pouch, 122
    enoki, **18**
    enoki, in no-fin shark
        fin soup, 42
    matsutake (pine), **20**
    pine, and shrimp soup, 47
    shiitake, **21**
    straw, **23**
mussels, in spicy
    seafood hot pot, 114–15
MUSTARD
    Chinese, **15**
    seeds, **11**
    spinach. *See* tatsoi

nam pla. *See* fish sauce
nam prik (nam phrik), **29**
napa cabbage, **21**.
    See also Chinese cabbage
Nepalese goat curry, *138*, 139
ngu vi huong, **11**.
    See also five-spice powder
no-fin shark fin soup, 42
NOODLES
    beef hor fan with prawns, 181
    beef pho', 48–49
    Chinese, **29**
    Japanese, **30**
    with kimchi in dried
        anchovy broth, 182–83
    pad Thai, 178
    pan mee, 176–77, *177*
    in spicy seafood hot pot, 114–15
    tan tan, 179
    vermicelli, wok-fried,
        with mushrooms and
        bean sprouts, 173
nori, **30**
nuoc mam. *See* fish sauce
nutmeg, **11**
nuts, in ice wine filling, 194–95